THE
PARABLES
OF CHANCE

JOHN NICHOLSON

Copyright © 2022 by John Nicholson

All rights reserved.

Book Cover design by: ebooklaunch.com

Back Cover Photo by: Brittany McLachlan Photography

Published in the United States

ISBN: 979-8-9873706-0-5

DEDICATION

On July 20, 2022, Oliver Dean Campbell made his official entrance into the world. There are numerous emotions that a parent experiences when their child has a baby. The delivery period has you anxious, as you pray that mother and baby will get through it safely. You keep vigilance on your phone, waiting for text updates from your son-in- in law Tim.

And then, the miracle is completed. He has arrived.

Oliver, I dedicate this novel to you. You see, you and this novel are both a new journey for me. I have put many hours into this book. And I look forward to spending many hours with you.

With much love,

Grandpa John

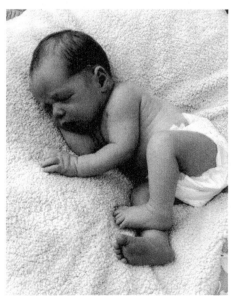

THE PARABLES OF CHANCE

INTRODUCTION

"You can't stop the future. You can't rewind the past. The only way to learn the secret ... is to press play," Jay Asher, Thirteen Reasons Why

"Things are about to change."

These words can evoke a variety of emotions, depending on who is saying them, and who is listening. Change can be viewed as both positive and negative. It can happen slowly over time, or it can occur in an instant. Many people say change is inevitable; others fight it for as long as possible.

The town of Parables was just such a place. Located in a scenic part of central Minnesota, it was a popular get-away for people living in the Twin Cities. Lakes, forests, and a small-town atmosphere allowed people to renew their spirits, as long as they left their modern conveniences unplugged, uncharged, and unanswered.

And when it came to change, the inhabitants of Parables felt no need of it. The gift shops sold articles that quoted some of the phrases that local writers had coined over the years. One of the favorites was posted under a silhouette of Parables: *If God does not change, why should we?"*
PSALM 55:19

1

But often change comes uninvited. No one anticipated what would happen back in 2011 when a major magazine selected Parables as "*One of Minnesota's Best Kept Secrets.*"

Suddenly Parables saw the influx of urbanization systemically squeeze out its charm, its innocence, and its values. The very things that made it the "best-kept secret" were becoming memories. The town found itself dealing with new problems, and tried to deal with the problems using old solutions.

Despite what was happening, the town's people hoped that somehow things would return to normal … *their normal.*

One event, one *parable* of sorts, created a ripple effect that extended outward, revealing the "new normal".

CHAPTER 1

The cat stood on his back legs so he could look out the window. He did not have much room. The car was full of boxes and other items that rattled and shifted each time they hit a bump. The rapid departure from the house left the cat, whose name was Tabby, confused and anxious.

Eventually, the car stopped at the side of the road. The driver got out and opened the door where Tabby was pinned. He fell out but managed to land safely.

A lifelong housecat, Tabby did not like this sudden adventure. The woman scooped up the cat and slammed the car door. Tabby flinched, then looked up at his owner who continued to look straight ahead, avoiding eye contact.

The woman kept a brisk pace as she entered a wooded area. She eventually stopped, removed the collar with the identification tag, and tossed the cat to the ground. The cat studied the unfamiliar surroundings. He saw a toad resting near a tree stump and approached it slowly to investigate. He gently touched it and watched as it jumped several times. Fascinated, he snuck up and touched it again. This time the toad hopped under a rotted log. Tabby reached under the log and tried to retrieve the toad, but it was beyond his reach.

He stopped when he heard the sound of the car driving away. By the time he ran to the road, the car was gone. He sat by the road, waiting for the woman to come back. Eventually, he fell asleep.

Tabby woke up when it started to rain. The light rain quickly turned into a downpour. Loud claps of thunder followed as the wind picked up. Terrified, Tabby sought shelter under a tree, as the rain pelted him with each surge of wind. At home he would hide under the bed until a storm subsided; now there was nowhere to take cover.

The lightning and thunder lessened after the initial downpour passed, but steady rain continued. Nightfall brought with it an early October chill. Tabby shivered as he tried to shake the moisture off his thin coat of fur. The relentless rain prevented him from finding any relief.

As conditions got worse, he decided not to wait any longer and started to try and find his way home.

Tabby walked along the busy road as he navigated his way toward Parables, hoping that each passing car was his owner. The bright lights and wet pavement made it hard to see the edge of the road. Drivers were caught off guard by a cat walking outside in a rainstorm. Most blew their horns, and several slammed on their brakes as he came into view at the last second.

A semi-truck hit a pothole, generating a geyser of mud and water that landed directly on Tabby. He shook it off as best he could, and kept going.

Several perilous hours passed before Tabby made it to the outskirts of Parables. The rain had finally stopped; occasional lightning still flashed off in the distance.

Like so many lost cats and dogs before him, Tabby had a sense of where his home was located. Tired, cold, and hungry, he continued the journey, eager to be reunited with his owner. A large frog hopped across the street in front of him, but Tabby had no interest in chasing him. His only goal was to reach his home as quickly as possible.

The street lights glowed brightly through the fog that settled over the town. The few cars out were hampered by poor visibility and drove slowly. Once again, several drivers nearly hit him.

None stopped to help the dirty, frightened cat.

As he crossed 4th street, Tabby saw something turn and head in his direction. At first whatever it was moved slowly. Then it broke into a run. A large feral cat cleared through the fog and blocked Tabby's progress.

The street-hardened beast let loose with an angry hiss, as he circled Tabby to size him up. Satisfied that he could make quick work of him, he attacked. Tabby, caught off guard, was slammed to the ground, as the feral cat scratched and bit him. The quiet of the night was interrupted by high-pitched screams of pain.

Tabby tried to fight back, but a lack of front claws combined with exhaustion made for little resistance. The feral cat leaned hard into him, easily pinning him down. Tabby fully extended his rear claws, flailing them wildly. He eventually was able to position a leg under his attacker and drag the claws across his inner thigh. The positioning of the feral cat allowed him to get a deep, penetrating strike. As the cat pulled the leg back, Tabby struck it again, creating a deeper wound. The feral cat retreated with a screech.

Tabby rolled over and tried to get away. But his attacker was not about to end the fight. Despite the wound, the feral cat hobbled after him. The two cats were bleeding, leaving spattered blood on the wet pavement. Tabby looked behind to see the angry cat quickly gaining ground. In no time, Tabby was once more slammed to the ground. The feral cat positioned himself so that Tabby could do no further damage.

Tabby's screeches caught the attention of a Rottweiler sleeping behind the fence where the attack was underway. The Rottweiler charged into the fog growling as he drew near to the source of the noise. He barked and snarled at the two cats, as he jumped and clawed at the fence. The feral cat, frightened by the menacing dog, jumped up and fled. Tabby, weakened by the attack, could only retreat slowly, enraging the Rottweiler, who snarled and barked as he followed the injured cat along the entire length of the fence.

The dog's owner turned on the back porch light and ran out to see what was causing the dog to react so violently. Unable to see anything in the fog, he ordered the dog into the house.

Silence returned to Parables, as an exhausted and battered cat continued his quest.

CHAPTER 2

Tabby no longer looked like a cute, handsome housecat. The blood from his wounds, along with mud and debris, covered his fur. The sun rose, and the fog lifted. Tabby felt vulnerable. He constantly scanned the area around him to see if the feral cat was back on his trail.

Somehow, despite the wounds and fatigue, he eventually found his house. He slowly climbed up the porch steps and pushed and pawed at the door. With no front claws, he barely made a sound.

Tabby whined a pitiful "meow" over and over again, hoping that the owner would hear him and open the door. When no one answered, he decided to make himself as comfortable as possible…and wait.

A car eventually pulled into the driveway. It was late afternoon, and Tabby arose from a fitful sleep. The sound of the car got him excited…his owner was back! He purred at the thought of her gathering him up, caring for his wounds, feeding him, and cuddling with him until he was warm again. He would let her know that he forgave her.

When a man emerged from the car, Tabby realized it was not his owner. The man who came out of the car seemed very angry when he saw the injured, dirty disheveled cat lying on the porch.

"Scat!" he yelled.

Tabby did not know what "Scat" meant. So, he stayed where he was, and waited for the man to open the door.

"Are you deaf, I said SCAT!!" he screamed.

When Tabby did not move, the man walked up and kicked Tabby as hard as he could. Tabby flew off the porch and landed awkwardly on the ground. He screeched in pain when the bone in his back right leg snapped.

Tabby looked up to see the man climbing down the porch, and advancing toward him. He somehow needed to get away. With a shot of pain, he hopped up on his three "good" legs and fled as best he could.

The man pursued Tabby, throwing rocks and screaming at him, to ensure the cat kept moving. Once he was satisfied the cat was gone, he turned and went inside the house.

Tabby crawled under some nearby bushes. No human had ever hurt him before.

"Who was this man, and what was he doing in his house?"

His thoughts turned to his other owner, the man whom he rarely saw anymore. A feeling of sadness came over Tabby as he thought of that owner, who would never do what this angry man had done.

Tabby's injured leg throbbed as he continuously tried to find a comfortable position under the bushes. Hungry and cold, he kept vigil for one or both owners to come home.

After several hours, the man staggered out of the house and down the steps. As he reached for his car keys, he spotted Tabby. He went back into the house and came back out with a broom.

"I said SCAT!!" he yelled.

Tabby awoke abruptly at the loud command of "SCAT". It meant that he had to move quickly, or the man would hurt him again. He slowly crawled out of the bushes and tried to move as fast as he could, despite the pain.

The man easily caught up to Tabby as he tried to get away. He raised the broom and swung it down hard on the struggling cat. The bristles bit into the side of Tabby's battered body, raking his wounds and knocking him over. Tabby whined as he struggled desperately to get back up.

The swinging motion of the broom threw the man off balance, and he fell sideways. Tabby was able to get a little separation before the man regained his balance. He was unable to protect the broken leg from the broom strike, and each bouncing motion sent jarring pain that almost made him stop. The man with the broom kept coming. Tabby sloshed through a puddle at the side of the driveway, as he struggled to keep moving.

The man gave up his pursuit once Tabby was off the property.

"Don't come back again" he yelled, "or I'll hit you with something a lot worse than a broom!"

CHAPTER 3

Tabby stopped once the pain became unbearable. He was relieved to see that the man was gone. He tried to lick some of the wounds that were bleeding. There were too many wounds and too little moisture in his mouth to do any good. The dehydrated cat gave up on the effort.

He started once again to move slowly, trying to keep from jarring the broken leg. Darkness was once more descending on Parables, along with the chilly temperatures. Tabby shivered. Weak, hungry, and harboring multiple injuries, the cold added to his misery. He was helpless and feared another attack from the cat or the man with the broom.

He stopped when he heard a rustling sound. A large mama raccoon and her babies were eating scraps of food from a fallen garbage can. Desperate for nourishment, Tabby decided to join them.

The mama raccoon hissed as Tabby approached, trying to warn him that he was getting too close to her babies. When Tabby continued to advance toward the scraps, she attacked.

The raccoon, strong and angry, easily defended her brood. She scratched and bit Tabby, who gave her no resistance. Once Tabby was motionless on the ground, she gathered up her babies, and left.

Tabby lay on the ground panting. The tip of his left ear was severed and bleeding. Twenty minutes passed, and he somehow got up. Now he was only able to drag his broken leg as he moved slowly along. He spotted a trash container behind a restaurant, crawled under it, and collapsed.

The cold, damp ground provided no comfort. His broken leg throbbed and twitched. His wounds oozed, draining his already depleted energy.

He would not be able to pull himself up again. A new pain hit; one that hurt much more than the feral cat's attack, or the man's kick, or the bristles on the broom, or the raccoon's bites.

He felt completely hopeless and alone.

In addition to his broken body, Tabby now had a broken heart.

He closed his eyes and felt himself fading away....

****

The last of the customers leaving the Creighton Family Restaurant zipped up their coats as they walked out into the cool night. They did not see the cat under the trash container, nor did they see the fox heading to the nearby park to hunt for rabbits, squirrels, or any other potential menu items.

The fox stopped when she smelled something under the garbage can. Spotting the cat, the fox elected to change her agenda. While a cat was normally not something a fox would hunt, this one was too easy to pass up. It would provide an easy meal for her hungry kits.

She pulled Tabby out by the scruff of his neck and sniffed him. He was still alive, despite all of his injuries. The fox picked up Tabby and prepared to shake out the remaining life so she could safely carry it back to her nearby den.

Suddenly the fox saw someone charging at her, yelling "SCAT!!!"

The fox dropped Tabby and ran away, but she did not go far. The human would surely leave soon, and she could return to the cat.

****

Tabby woke up slightly when the fox dropped him. He heard the word "SCAT!!!," and that meant someone was coming to hurt him again.

He could not move, or cry, or hope for mercy.

So, Tabby just closed his eyes, let out a soft whine, and waited for the hurt.

CHAPTER 4

Lizzy Candone, a waitress at the Creighton Family Restaurant, shuddered as she inspected the cat. Despite the horrible wounds, he was still breathing. Running to her car, she retrieved a blanket, and carefully placed the cat on it. Tabby's broken leg began to quiver; she worried that the cat was going into shock. He needed immediate help, and she did not want to drive to the hospital alone, especially with all of his injuries.

She pulled out her phone.

"Hello?" a tired voice answered.

"Ben, it's Lizzy. I need your help!"

"Are you OK Liz?" Ben asked. "What's going on?"

Lizzy relayed the situation.

Ben Odim turned on the phone's speaker so he could dress quickly. Fortunately, he had just gone to bed after finishing his accounting homework. He threw on his jeans and retrieved his auto parts work shirt from the hamper.

"Liz, I'm on my way," Ben said. "If that fox comes back, or any animal for that matter, you need to get away from the cat!"

Ben arrived within five minutes. He and Lizzy carefully loaded Tabby into the back seat. Tabby moaned every time Ben's car hit a bump.

"Easy Ben, he's hurting!" Lizzy lamented.

Marge Sutter, the receptionist, looked up as Lizzy and Ben rushed up to the counter. The animal hospital was two hours past closing time, but the staff was still working due to several emergency surgeries.

Marge had forgotten to lock the doors.

"How can I help you?" Marge asked, loud enough for the staff in back to know that there would be one more patient to service.

Lizzy quickly told how she had found the cat outside the restaurant where she worked, as it was being attacked by a fox. She then pulled back the blanket covering Tabby. The light provided a clearer view; Lizzy saw the injuries were much worse than she first thought.

Marge cringed. she had seen many animals over the years: sick animals, hurt animals and abused animals. She took a deep breath and looked directly at Lizzy.

"Would you mind telling me what really happened?" Marge asked tensely. "The fox story is not going to work."

The emotions of the night had been welling up, and for Lizzy, a line had just been crossed. This woman had implied the one thing that guaranteed to get Lizzy's blood boiling: that she abused the cat.

Lizzy gently handed Tabby to Ben, and then returned to Marge.

"Would you mind telling me what you're insinuating?" Lizzy replied as she drew closer to Marge. "If you were hired to dole out sick accusations, you're doing fantastic. But you clearly have no clue how to do your job, and I don't have to defend myself with some minimum wage hack!"

The stinging remarks were delivered a short distance from Marge's face. She picked up her phone.

"Back off!" she said, "unless you want to spend the night in lockup!"

Unfazed, Lizzy pulled out her phone and dialed nine, then one.

"I just need to dial the final number, and we both get to go to lockup!" Lizzy sneered. "Maybe we can share a cell!"

Susan McNamara, the veterinarian, ran to the front when she heard the commotion. Like a seasoned hockey referee, she slid in between the combatants, separating them with outstretched arms. She ordered Lizzy and Marge to calm down and put their phones away, as Ben pulled Lizzy back while trying to hold the cat.

The two glared at each other as they shut down their phones. Lizzy turned to Ben, who refused to hand over the cat. Marge unknowingly brought Lizzy back to unresolved issues; Ben knew she needed time to defuse.

Susan led Ben and Lizzy to an exam room. Ben gently put Tabby on the table and pulled back the blanket. It was the first time Ben got a good look at the damage Tabby sustained. He now understood Marge's reaction.

Susan brought Ben and Lizzy into the reception area. After formal introductions, Susan asked Lizzy to tell her everything she knew about the cat, which took less than two minutes.

"OK," Susan said, "wait here; I'll come to get you once the exam is over."

In the exam room, Tabby remained motionless as students cleaned the bites and scratches. The deeper wounds bled slightly. The IV hookup was a challenge. A wave of relief went through the room when the fifth attempt was successful, and the fluids and pain medication slowly entered the emaciated cat.

Susan entered the exam room and closed the door behind her. The students gave their reports, while they continued tending to the cat. Susan approached the table, shaking her head as she initiated her exam.

"Whatever happened to you, poor little cat?" she thought. The damage was heartbreaking, even to a seasoned veterinarian.

Tabby flinched as Susan gently moved his broken leg. The forensic side of Susan's personality began to surmise what likely happened. A break this severe would have left the cat defenseless. The lack of claws in front further depleted his abilities to fight off his attackers. The force of the blow that broke his leg meant he likely took a direct hit from someone he trusted. There was no chip; all the signs were there that this cat was a "lover, not a fighter." He had little if any street smarts.

The pain he was enduring was intense. The cat, she thought, would have been better off if the fox had finished him off.

Susan removed her exam gloves and asked Ben and Lizzy to come into her office. Lizzy shot another glare at Marge as they passed her desk; Ben grabbed her hand in case Lizzy tried to change directions.

Susan directed Lizzy and Ben to have a seat as she closed the door.

"First of all, Lizzy, I know you did not have anything to do with what happened to that cat," Susan said. "But Marge is right about one thing. That cat has been abused. He's in bad shape."

Susan put her notes on the desk, shook her head, took a deep breath, and began her assessment.

"His leg is badly broken and needs immediate surgery if we hope to save it. He has lost a lot of blood and is severely dehydrated. There are extensive wounds that need to be treated; some will require stitches. We would also need to conduct further tests to see if any internal injuries need to be addressed. In addition to the medications, he will need vaccines and antibiotics. The cat does not have a chip, so we have no way of knowing his health history. If he survived the surgery, he would have a long, difficult recovery. This will all be very costly, and it may accomplish nothing more than to prolong his agony. Even if he did survive, we do not know how all this will impact him emotionally. In my opinion, the humane thing to do is euthanize and relieve his suffering."

Ben held Lizzy's hand. In his mind, this was a logical assessment; but it was Lizzy's decision.

"Can I see him?" Lizzy asked.

"Of course, give us a few moments to finish up, and then I'll take you back," Susan said.

Everyone assumed that Lizzy wanted to say goodbye to the cat. They cleaned him up as best they could, then left when Lizzy entered the room.

She walked quietly over to the table, bent over, and gently stroked Tabby on the head. He opened his eyes slightly, as Lizzy talked softly to him. He then drifted back into unconsciousness.

Lizzy exited the exam room. Ben followed her as she walked up to Susan.

"Please do whatever needs to be done to try and save him," Lizzy said.

Susan sighed. It had been a long day, and this was not how she hoped it would end.

"Let's go back to my office," she said.

Susan once again went over what they knew about the cat, and also what they did not know. She wanted to make sure Lizzy understood what she was asking, along with all the potential consequences.

"I want to give him a chance," Lizzy said when Susan finished.

Susan sighed again.

"Well then, we will need a deposit to cover the costs," Susan said.

"Very well; how much do you need?" Lizzy asked.

Susan wrote down the estimated charges and slid the paper across the desk.

Lizzy flinched. After a few moments, she reached into her purse and pulled out her charge card.

"Marge will handle the payment and paperwork, just give her the sheet," Susan said as she rose to leave the office. "I hope you reconsider."

Lizzy went over to the reception desk, where Marge completed the paperwork and processed the down payment. Once everything was completed, Marge held out the charge card.

Lizzy snatched the card out of Marge's hand, turned, and started to walk out with Ben.

Susan intercepted them before they left.

"Don't ever do that again," Susan said firmly, "or you will have to take your cat to another vet."

Lizzy nodded and then left with Ben.

During the ride back to the Creighton Family Restaurant, Lizzy replayed the whole night in her mind. She had dragged her boyfriend out of bed, to help rescue a cat that would likely die. She got into a tense argument with a woman who was old enough to be a grandmother. And to top it all off, she added hundreds of dollars to a nearly maxed-out credit card, just as a new round of nursing school expenses were about to hit.

"Do you think I'm being foolish?" Lizzy asked.

"No!" Ben replied, "Crazy maybe, but not foolish," he said with a smile.

Lizzy rested her head on Ben's shoulder and thanked him for helping her. She kissed him when they reached the restaurant parking lot. As she neared her car, she turned and asked Ben, "What did I just do?"

Ben could only shrug his shoulders.

CHAPTER 5

Ruth Lambert's brain was on overdrive, fueled by a ceaseless rage that started the day she found out her husband Tony was having an affair. She never saw it coming.

Or perhaps, she never wanted to see it coming.

Ruth played the day back in her mind over and over again. She arrived home from the infertility center, chastising Tony that if he was not going to be a more "active participant," they were spending a lot of money for nothing.

"Do you or do you not want me to have a baby?" she asked.

Tony never answered, and he did not look at her. Instead, he confessed that a coworker named Olivia Sky was pregnant, and he was the father.

The news hit Ruth hard. Had Tony gotten tired of waiting for science to provide the child he so desperately wanted? Or perhaps he just got tired of Ruth? Whatever the reason, Ruth felt betrayed in every way possible.

The divorce was the kind everyone said you should avoid: "messy." Ruth fought over everything: the house, money, cars, household items; nothing was settled amicably.

Ted Logan presided over the divorce proceedings. He was a long-time judge in Parables and was known for trying to settle cases as quickly as possible, so people could rebuild their lives. But this divorce drained the judge and everyone associated with it. The attorneys on both sides tried desperately to settle the couple's issues, but Ruth refuted most offers, no matter how reasonable. Even Judge Logan's patience and calm demeanor could not lessen Ruth's rage from adding fuel to the inferno. She was doing everything in her power to make sure Tony's departure was a nightmare.

One of the final battles was over Tabby.

Tabby originally belonged to Tony's mom, Beverly, who was a widow. The cat was a faithful and loving companion to Beverly, especially during her battle with terminal breast cancer.

As the cancer progressed, Tabby's role in Beverly's care grew more important. Beverly called Tabby her "hospice" cat who helped her navigate the final painful days with his constant vigil.

Shortly before she died, Beverly called Tony and Ruth into her room and asked them to sit down. She was stroking Tabby, who was lying at her side.

"I hope I can impose on you both with a final request," Beverly said.

"Sure," Tony said, "anything Mom."

"Could you please take Tabby after I'm gone, and provide him with a good home?"

When they both gladly accepted the request, a look of peace came over Beverly's face. She took both of their hands, and with tears told them over and over again how happy she was that Tabby would have a good home once she was gone.

She passed away peacefully two days later.

Now, as the divorce proceedings were finally winding down, Tony hoped that Ruth would relinquish Tabby to him since it was his mom's cat. He also thought the judge would give him custody once he was aware of Tabby's history. So Tony was caught off guard by Ruth's accusation that Tony regularly abused Tabby. He quickly tried to defend himself.

"I would never do anything to hurt Tabby!" Tony objected. "I love him."

Ruth quickly interjected. "You loved Tabby the same as you loved me!" she screamed.

Tears and hysteria were easily produced by Ruth. She begged Judge Logan not to take the cat away from her. Tony had already ruined her life, and Tabby was her only solace.

"His whore will use Tabby to drive another stake in my heart!" Ruth wailed while pointing at Olivia.

The judge, tired of all the bickering, awarded Ruth full custody. Tony was allowed supervised visits. His arguments for unsupervised visits fell on deaf ears. Olivia wished that the judge denied Tony any visitations. She wanted him to avoid any contact with Ruth once this mess was done.

Shortly after the divorce was finalized, the house was sold, and Ruth packed up her car with odds and ends that she would need until the movers delivered her other belongings. She located an apartment in Newton Bay, a town 28 miles from Parables; far enough to try and start a new life.

There was one thing left to do as she left the house that she once shared with Tony.

Shortly after leaving Tabby in the woods, she mulled over what to tell her ex about his beloved cat. What would hurt him the most? She decided on telling him that Tabby had somehow escaped while she was moving into her new apartment. She had looked everywhere, but he was nowhere to be found.

The approaching rainstorm disrupted her raging thoughts. When the thunder and lightning started, she pulled the car over.

For the first time, Ruth thought about Tabby, and how terrified he must be. She pictured him wandering in the woods, alone and afraid. He hated thunderstorms. He might panic and run out into the road.

She remembered her mother-in-law Beverly, picturing her smile as she thanked Ruth and Tony repeatedly for taking Tabby. Ruth loved Beverly. She was always good to her. Beverly would certainly be upset with Tony for his adultery, but she would be horrified to know what Ruth had done to Tabby.

She turned the car around, hoping she could find the area where she released him. She made random stops where she thought she had let him go. At each stop, she parked the car, got out, and peered into the darkness. The flashlight she had was practically useless; the batteries were almost dead. As she searched each area, Ruth called his name over and over.

"Tabby! Here Tabby! Come Tabby....please!"

She desperately wanted to find him now, but each attempt was met with the same result: silence.

CHAPTER 6

Officer Riley was returning to the station when he saw a car parked on the side of the road. He turned around to check it out. The radio crackled as he called in the license plate and the location of the vehicle, as the LED lights recently installed on his vehicle lit up the night. Riley walked around the vehicle, looking inside with his flashlight. It was filled with belongings and was left unlocked. The station radioed back that the car was not reported stolen, and the owner was named Ruth Lambert.

After several minutes, Officer Riley heard something. He turned his flashlight and saw Ruth walking toward the car.

"Miss, are you Ruth Lambert, the owner of this car?" he asked.

"Yes officer, that's me," Ruth replied.

"Is there anyone else with you?" Riley asked.

"No…just me," Ruth said sheepishly.

He asked to see her license, registration, and proof of insurance. Ruth had to remove items from the front seat so she could search the glove compartment. Officer Riley told Ruth to get back into her car while he checked out the information. After he verified everything with the station, he returned and handed the information back to her.

"You sure have this vehicle packed to the hilt!" Riley said. "Do you mind if I ask why you are out walking this late at night during a rainstorm, navigating the woods with a flashlight that's barely lit?"

"Well," Ruth said in a quiet voice, "I hate to admit this, but I had to pee."

Riley nodded. "And the car; you do know you are supposed to be able to see out the back window? At this time of night, a deer or other animal could jump out on the road without warning. The way this car is packed, that microwave could fly forward and kill you."

Ruth apologized. She told the officer about her recent divorce, the sale of the house, and her new apartment in Newton Bay. Riley heard the emptiness in her voice and saw the sadness in her eyes, far different from the smiling picture on her driver's license.

"Well Ms. Lambert, you're obviously under a great deal of stress." he sighed. "Please be honest with me…were you planning to hurt yourself?"

"No!" Ruth stammered. "Why would you ask me that?"

"Well," he said, "You're not all that far from a public washroom. You walked quite a distance into the woods. Although I don't see any weapons or pills in your possession, I had to ask, in case you needed help."

"No, really, I'm fine," Ruth said, hoping she sounded convincing.

Officer Riley rearranged some of the items in the back seat so the view out of the back window was clear. He reminded her to use her flashers next time and to replace the batteries in her flashlight.

"Drive carefully and take care of yourself! It would be a good idea to seek some counseling once you get settled. Don't be afraid to ask for help."

Ruth nodded. She thanked Officer Riley for his help and then drove away.

Riley returned to his squad car and radioed in that he was going to do a quick search of the area. He walked into the woods where he had seen Ruth emerge, shining the flashlight back and forth. He picked up Ruth's footprints in a muddy patch, well past a distance that provided adequate cover for relieving herself.

After a long career in law enforcement, Riley's experience told him something else was going on with Ruth.

And while he was not certain, he thought he heard Ruth calling someone while he was looking over her car.

CHAPTER 7

Ruth dialed Tony's number and waited for it to go to voicemail. She knew he would not answer once he looked at the caller ID.

"Tony, this is Ruth. I'm at my apartment, and I can't find Tabby. I was busy moving things and he must have slipped out of the door. I'll call if he turns up."

Tony called back immediately, demanding more information.

"I don't know what else to tell you. He's been gone for three days." Ruth said.

"Three days!! And you're only letting me know now?" Tony seethed. "Did you check with your neighbors? Did you leave his food outside, or check with animal control?! Damn it, Ruth, you know as well as I do, he's a house cat! You need to…"

Ruth interrupted his inquiries.

"Listen, he's your cat too. You can look for him and do all those things. I'm still trying to get settled in. If he turns up, I'll give you a call."

"Wait!" Tony said in an exasperated voice. "I am going to search for him, and put up some posters to see if anyone might have seen him."

Olivia Sky, Tony's pregnant mistress, blew up when she heard what Tony said.

"No, you won't! I don't want you to go anywhere near that bitch!" she yelled loudly, hoping that Ruth would hear.

Tony ended the call.

The plan that Ruth had carefully orchestrated was working perfectly, yet she no longer had the appetite for it. The sweet taste of revenge was now bitter. The endless fights, costly court battles, and the demise of an innocent cat left her feeling numb.

Intense loneliness enveloped her. She crawled into bed fully dressed, slowly drifting into a fitful sleep, wishing things were different.

****

The next day Tony and Olivia drove to Newton Bay. Tony put up posters offering a $500 reward. Each poster had tabs listing Tony's name and phone number. As he put up the posters, he periodically called out Tabby's name.

After two hours, Olivia had enough.

"There are enough posters," Olivia said. "I want to leave; my back is killing me!"

On the long ride home, Olivia demanded that Tony shift his focus to her and the baby. This new development left her feeling exasperated, and fearful that the divorce drama was now entering a different phase.

"When will it finally be over?" She wondered.

CHAPTER 8

Promises flowed like water from the mouth of Rick Carver after he convinced his wife Shirley that they needed to buy a house. He assured her that this time he was serious about getting his act together. He would get the drinking under control, as well as his temper. He would become the father that their son Matt deserved. He did not doubt that everything he pledged would become a reality.

But once again, his actions were beginning to prove otherwise.

Matt and Shirley were at their old apartment, gathering up the last of their belongings. Rick paid a visit to his favorite "watering hole" since he had some time before the movers arrived.

"The moment calls for some light celebrating." He reasoned.

The bartender at Nelson's Sports Lounge was not excited to see Rick walk in and order a drink. He was becoming more and more of a problem, and the lounge could certainly do without his business.

As if on cue, Rick took exception to someone mocking the Vikings and their "empty" Super Bowl trophy case. The patron behind the comment was wearing a Packers jersey.

"You know what cheese head?" Rick yelled as he approached the man. "You're a loser, along with the whole state of Wisconsin. You need to go back across the river, so we don't have to listen to your BS!!"

"I'm not talking to you, so mind your own business!" the man yelled back.

It did not take long for the alcohol-fueled argument to escalate. Soon, names and curse words were flying. The rest of the lounge fell silent as customers stopped and nervously watched the engagement.

Rick suddenly grabbed his verbal opponent by his jersey. "You owe everyone in here an apology!" Rick demanded.

The bartender yelled for the manager, who was a former Marine named Mike. Mike ran up from the room in the back and went into bouncer mode. He put a choke hold on Rick and separated him from the other man. Rick's arms and legs were lifted off of the ground as he was carried toward the door. Rick kicked the marine's leg; it was a big mistake.

Slamming Rick to the ground, Mike grabbed Rick's ear and twisted it.

"You do that again, and your ear comes off!"

As they exited the door, Rick was once again thrown down to the ground. The manager then administered a retaliatory kick to Rick's leg that sent pain shooting down his side. Before Rick could react, the manager grabbed him by his hair and held a fist in front of his bleeding nose.

"Get out of here now! Don't ever come here again! If you do, you better be ready to spend some time in jail."

Rick knew this was no idle threat. The police were well aware that he was a problem child. He got up and staggered away, and went to a nearby gas station to clean up.

The clerk at the register grimaced. The restroom he had just cleaned was about to be soiled. He hoped Rick did not puke; his minimum wage job had enough challenges.

Rick felt lucky that nothing was broken. He rinsed off his face and used a pile of towels to wipe away the blood. When he came out, the clerk was glaring at him in disgust.

"You got a problem?" Rick growled.

The store clerk pointed to the security camera above the sign assuring full prosecution of any criminal acts. Rick waved to the camera, kicked the door open, and left.

He went to the new Walmart in town and purchased a towel and some shower supplies. The clerk who checked him out was frightened when she saw that Rick's shirt was spattered with blood. Rick felt a myriad of other eyes also looking at him.

He was failing again.

Why did he just get into a bar fight?

And why did that stupid cat have to set him off yesterday?

He found himself wrestling with his conscience as he tried to justify his actions. The cat was a stray. It might have had rabies. And besides, the cat refused to leave, so in essence, the cat asked for it.

As for the bar fight, all the idiot needed to do was shut up and apologize. Now, Rick was forced to find a new watering hole.

Rick's conscience, though severely damaged, wasn't buying his lies. The guy in the bar was not even talking to him. The cat was harmless. It was badly hurt and in need of help. He was an easy target for Rick's rage, and Rick let him endure the full brunt of it.

A pattern was developing that Rick refused to acknowledge. The drinking and the anger were working in tandem. His latest battle with his conscience was interrupted when his phone rang. It was his wife, Shirley.

"Hi honey, how are you this fine day?" Rick said in his most flattering voice.

"I'm fine Rick," Shirley said suspiciously. "Have you heard from the movers?"

"Yes, they will be here tomorrow, around 2:00 pm."

"Good," Shirley replied. "Make sure they're careful. Most of the boxes are marked, so make sure they put them in the right rooms. My dad offered to help once the movers arrive."

Rick's father-in-law made it clear on several occasions that he was worried about Rick's drinking. Rick assured him that he had it under control. His father-in-law, like other people in Rick's life, was not buying it. Rick knew the move was just another opportunity for Shirley's dad to chat with him about getting help.

"No, I'll be fine," Rick said to Shirley. "If I need any help, I'll have Bill give me a hand."

Shirley sighed. She desperately wanted to maintain a positive outlook.

"OK fine," Shirley said. "But if Bill has been drinking, I don't want him handling my china or any other fragile items!"

"You have my word," Rick said. "Enjoy your time with Matt. We will all be busy the next couple of weeks. Tell Matt the yard is great. We have plenty of room to play catch and work on his curve ball."

Shirley hoped this was not another one of Rick's empty promises. She told Rick that she loved him as she hung up the phone.

Rick went back to the house and fell asleep on the air mattress. He woke up the next day with a terrible hangover. The movers called to say they would arrive in 2 hours.

"Perfect." Rick thought. "Enough time for a few cocktails to take the edge off."

CHAPTER 9

Susan McNamara was upset. The veterinarian had seen too many cases like Tabby. The odds of survival were slim. Yet she was instructed to do everything to save him.

The surgery was long and difficult, requiring the placement of screws and a metal plate into Tabby's leg. He survived, but the procedure left him very weak. The cat would need to wear a cast for several weeks to keep the leg immobilized. During that time, a host of complications could arise.

"My poor friend, please forgive me," Susan said as she examined Tabby. "I hope we are not doing this all in vain."

X-rays, surgery, and medications were quickly ramping up the bill. Susan told Marge to call Lizzy and let her know the leg surgery was over and to inform her that an additional payment was required.

Marge smiled as she dialed the phone.

"Hello, may I speak to Elizabeth Can-don-ee?" Marge asked.

"It's Candone, two syllables, not three," Lizzy said sarcastically. "And I have not been called Elizabeth since kindergarten."

Marge feigned a professional response.

"Ok, sorry; duly noted," Marge said. "This is Marge from the animal hospital. I was calling to inform you that the surgery on your cat is over. He should be awake in a few hours. We will need an additional payment for the surgery and other services. I can go over this with you when you come in."

Lizzy sighed. "OK, can you tell me what the balance is at this point?"

"The balance is $2,183. This is in addition to the $700 you already paid." Marge said.

Lizzy paused, and then said, "I'll be there in about two hours."

Marge opened the file for **CANDONE CAT**. "We don't have a name for your cat," Marge said. "Do you have one in mind, or should I just leave it blank?"

"Put down Chance," Lizzy replied.

"OK," Marge replied. "That's one syllable, right?"

"Yes, it is. I'm sensing you need a good comedy therapist." Lizzy said. "Let me know if you want a referral."

Lizzy sat holding her head in her hands, wondering what she was doing. At a time when her finances could not be tighter, she had taken on the quest to save this cat. Ask a hundred people if they thought she should let Chance go, and ninety-nine would say yes.

But there was something that she saw in Chance when she was alone with him in the exam room. Something that told her to continue the fight, even if it appeared that Chance no longer wanted to fight.

She could not give up; not yet.

CHAPTER 10

Lizzy gently stroked Chance. The surgery was over, but she wondered if it was too little, too late. In addition to the cast on his leg, Chance had stitches and bandages for his wounds. Part of his left ear had to be removed, and a cone was placed around his head. His breathing was labored as he slept in the recovery kennel. He looked like a macabre science experiment.

But somehow, he was still alive.

"Keep fighting Chance," Lizzy whispered as she left the room.

She brought her payment to Marge, and then met with Susan to discuss a possible installment plan. Susan explained that while sympathetic to Lizzy's financial situation, she had a business to run. Marge set up the installment plan, which included interest, as well as penalties for late payments.

Lizzy took the pen from Marge and signed it.

Later that day, Lizzy did the math; she could not make the monthly vet payments and still cover her rent and nursing school expenses. Her finances were maxed out, and her credit rating would plummet if a single payment was missed. That in turn could jeopardize her job search once she graduated.

Despite only having one semester and clinicals left to complete, she made the difficult decision to put nursing school on hold.

She left the vet hospital and went to her apartment before her shift started at the Creighton Family Restaurant. The box marked "Max" was in the back of her closet. She pulled it out and removed the contents. A litter box, a scratching post, some cat toys, and two food bowls rounded out the remnants from her days with Max.

Lizzy took down the picture of Max that was stationed next to his ashes on the mantle. The memory of his demise came flooding back. It was years since it happened, but the wounds were still fresh.

Max was a large, gray cat, who did not like to remain in the apartment at night, especially if Lizzy was at school or working late at the restaurant. He would patrol the area around the apartment building, protecting it from mice and other potential invaders.

Lizzy would cringe when Max was at the door waiting for her with his latest offering. Of course, Max would be pleased with himself, despite Lizzy's disgust as she disposed of the gift.

Lizzy loved Max. He would always come to her when she called his name. He enjoyed being stroked as Lizzy studied her assignments. His relentless purring assured her that he was grateful for all that she did for him.

She found Max in a shelter shortly before he was scheduled to be euthanized. Max was shaking in his cage as if he knew his time was short. Lizzy stopped when she walked by Max, and he reached his paw through the cage. They connected immediately.

Eventually, everyone in the building and the surrounding neighborhood knew Max. He trusted everyone, and especially enjoyed it when children would call his name and pet him. People said he acted more like a dog than a cat.

At the end of a long day of work and school, Lizzy looked forward to coming home and seeing Max waiting for her. Once she was home, Max was content to remain indoors so he could enjoy her attention.

And then, one night, his trusting attitude cost him dearly.

Lizzy had just taken her exams for the semester and was looking forward to spending a quiet evening in her apartment with Max, so she could relax and unwind. She was on the phone with Ben, when she noticed something near the apartment door. As she got closer, she screamed into the phone.

There, a few feet from the apartment entrance lay Max. His battered body was splattered with paintball pellets. The grimace on his face and shallow breathing revealed the pain he was suffering. Despite his injuries, Max had somehow dragged himself to the apartment door.

Ben raced over to the apartment and helped Lizzy climb into the car as she held Max. They drove at high speed to the Veterinary hospital, where he was rushed into an exam room.

The staff worked on Max for half an hour before he died.

Lizzy screamed when they gave her the news. She sobbed as she got a close look at the mangled body of her beloved pet.

Ben called the police when they returned to Lizzy's apartment. Police officer immediately came to the apartment to document what happened.

"Unfortunately, this is part of an ugly pattern." The officer said. "Whoever is doing this must be stopped."

The boys, all juveniles, were eventually caught when they became more daring and less cautious. They appeared before Judge Logan, an avid animal lover. The police compiled a list of animals victimized by the boys; with twenty-three incidents in all. Fourteen of the pets died from the attacks, and the remainder were seriously injured. The judge assigned each boy to twenty-three weekends of community service, which consisted of cleaning litter from streets and highways for eight hours. Any reports of slacking meant they would not get credit for that weekend.

After ten weekends, Judge Logan summoned the boys back to court. He wanted them to face the victims of their crimes.

All twenty-three victims showed up.

Each victim had a chance to question the boys, and to tell them how their actions affected their lives. When it was Lizzy's turn, she told them that she was a nursing student. She told them about Max's history, and how much he meant to her throughout the years. She told how when she examined her friend after he died, she found fractured bones, injuries to his eyes, and signs of internal bleeding.

He also had a broken back.

"So," Lizzy asked, "why did you target him? Why did you have to make sure he was hit on every inch of his body? And when did you decide it was time to stop?"

As with other victims, the boys looked down, reluctant to answer.

One of them however was trying unsuccessfully not to smile. The one named Lance Dennison.

"Boys, I'm not going to tell you again!" yelled Judge Logan. "Answer the questions, speak clearly, and look at the person asking the questions!"

"We lured him with treats." One boy said. "Once he was close enough…"

The boy paused and then continued.

"Lance hit him in the back with a two-by-four. He made us wait until the cat started crawling away on his front paws, and then we shot him with the paintball guns."

Lance looked up at the boy. He shot him a look that made it clear he was angry.

A female officer held Lizzy back as she tried to rush at the boys, fists clenched.

"You're worthless pieces of @#!" Lizzy screamed. "Max would have come to you without any treats! He crawled home after you tortured him. He died in agony!"

Each victim waited for the opportunity to come forward and confront the boys.

One of the last to get her chance to speak was a six-year-old girl, whose Jack Russell had to be put down due to the severity of the injuries inflicted by the boys.

Her voice shook as she told the boys how much she loved Rusty, and how much she missed him. She told about the tricks he could do, and how she would dress him up to have make-believe tea. She stopped occasionally to wipe her tears, while her parents stood at her side, glaring at the boys.

Amy had only one question for the boys.

"Why did you do it?"

Once again, the boys were silent. None of them offered an answer, so an angry Judge Logan intervened once more.

"Boys, I'm going to give you fifteen seconds to give this poor girl a legitimate answer, or I may have to take a recess, along with these fine police officers, and leave you alone with these people!"

Lance lifted his head and looked directly at Amy.

"We thought it was fun!" he said, as he put a smile on his face.

Amy began to shake. How could he say it was fun? Her grief was now compounded by terror. Her mom covered her face, as her father and other parents lurched forward in anger.

"Sorry folks, but it was the judge's order!" Lance announced as he was led out of the courtroom.

Judge Logan met privately with the boys, hoping that the session with the victims got through to them. He offered to reduce their community service if they agreed to attend counseling and write letters of apology to each of the victims. They agreed to do it.

One morning Amy's father saw the boys working on the side of Highway 8. He pulled over, and before the guards knew what was happening, he confronted Lance. Lance punched the father, and then mocked him and his daughter. The punches flew, and Lance suddenly *allowed* the father to hit him in the face. The guards pulled the father off, as Lance fell to the ground and feigned unconsciousness.

Once at the hospital, Lance called his mother. She hired a lawyer who initiated a lawsuit. After a preliminary hearing, the judge was instructed by the city lawyer to cut Lance free, in exchange for the lawsuit being dropped. Lance appeared at the hearing, smiling at the judge the entire time.

The judge had hoped to reach the boy, but Lance had no remorse for what he did. It became clear that any righteous qualities were systemically beaten out of him. He lost all respect for the agencies and entities who failed to rescue him from the abuse. This included his mother; *especially* his mother.

But there were times when her overwhelming guilt came in handy.

Despite the time that had passed and the capture and punishment of the boys, Lizzy still blamed herself for what happened to Max. She should have left to go home right after her exams instead of stopping to celebrate with her nursing school friends.

He might, she brooded, still be alive.

Ben, her boyfriend, served as her counselor, constantly assuring her that nothing was farther from the truth. Max perished because of an act of brutality, not because of anything Lizzy did or did not do.

Now Lizzy found Chance, and in her mind, he was redemption for Max. A twisted view perhaps, but she was determined to do all she could to save him.

Whatever the cost ...

CHAPTER 11

Ruth could not stop thinking about Tabby. The new apartment in Newton Bay was quiet and lonely. It was not the oasis of peace that she longed for. Tabby would have been good company, curiously searching the new premises, and bidding for her attention as she unpacked.

He was an innocent victim. The deed was done, but the turmoil was an unplanned development. She woke each morning exhausted, as vivid dreams disrupted her sleep. While the scenarios changed, they usually ended with Tabby dying in her arms. His eyes had the same look as when she left him in the woods. The message in those eyes was clear: *"I don't understand, I trusted you! I loved you!"*

She wanted to continue to search, but if she was found again by the police, they would suspect something was going on besides "nature's call."

There was one more possibility, although a slim one.

On the drive back to the old house, Ruth cringed each time she saw the remains of a dead animal. None appeared to be Tabby, so she continued to hope that somehow, he found his way back. There were, after all, stories of pets traveling long distances to be reunited with their owners.

The "For Sale" sign with "SOLD" on top was still at the front of the driveway. Ruth was reminded that not so long ago this was her house, and now the dreams it once held were officially over.

She rang the bell and heard the familiar chime.

"I'll get it!" yelled Matt as he raced to greet their first visitor.

Ruth took a deep breath as the door swung open, hoping she did not look like a complete basket case.

"Hi, I'm Ruth, the prior owner of this house," she said. "I'm wondering if I could speak with one of your parents."

"Sure, my mom is home!" Matt replied. "Mom, a lady wants to talk to you!" he yelled.

Shirley left the box she was unpacking in the kitchen and went to see who was at the door. She smiled as she recognized Ruth and invited her in.

"I'm sorry I don't have anything to offer you," Shirley said. "I still have a lot of unpacking to do, and I have not had time to go to the store. I can offer you a glass of water if you like."

"No thanks," Ruth replied. "I'm sorry to interrupt you. It won't take long. I came back in the hopes that you might have seen my cat. His name is Tabby."

Matt listened intently as Ruth told of Tabby's "escape." When Ruth started to tear up, Matt's ten-year-old heart had a surging desire to somehow help her.

"Do you have a picture of your cat?" Matt asked.

"Why yes, I do!" Ruth said, hoping that Matt might have seen him.

Matt was studying the picture when Rick walked in the door. Shirley was angry that he left her and Matt to handle the unpacking, while he went out to tend to some unexplained business.

That argument would have to be put on hold.

"Rick, this is Ruth," Shirley said. "You may have remembered her from the closing?"

"Oh, yes, hello," Rick said, his words slurred.

"Ruth, my husband has been here at the house quite a lot since the closing. Please tell him about your cat."

Ruth repeated her story, trying to be careful that she told the same version. The tears that trickled down seemed to flow from a heartbroken cat owner, and not from a guilty conscience.

When she finished, she wiped her eyes with the tissue Shirley had provided. Matt walked over to his dad.

"Here is a picture of the cat, Dad. He looks friendly. Did you happen to see him around?"

Rick knew instantly that the cat in the picture was the one he viciously attacked. It seemed as if the cat was looking right at him.

Shirley knew Rick was intoxicated. He was also acting uneasy as he denied seeing the cat. Her instincts told her that Rick knew something. She hoped he was telling the truth, but....

Ruth gave Shirley her phone number and left some of Tabby's treats and food in case he happened to return. She began sobbing again when Shirley hugged her.

"Rick, make yourself useful and move some boxes so that Ruth can sit on the sofa," Shirley said.

Gradually, Ruth was able to compose herself. She apologized and thanked the family for their time.

"Would you mind if I keep this picture, so we know what Tabby looks like?" Matt asked as Ruth prepared to leave.

"Certainly," Ruth said as she wiped her eyes and attempted a smile. "I have others." She thanked everyone again, wished them well in their new house, and left.

CHAPTER 12

Matt studied the picture. The lost cat was being held by two people who were smiling. One was Ruth, the lady who had just left. The other must have been her ex-husband. Matt's mom explained to him that the house they had just bought was available because the prior owners were getting a divorce.

Matt thought Ruth looked pretty when she smiled. She did not look like that same woman today. The heartache of losing both her cat and her marriage must be terrible. The tears Ruth shed revealed a deep pain that Matt was familiar with. He had two close friends that went through the divorces of their parents. Matt hated how much it hurt them and changed their lives. He now realized that adults involved in a divorce also suffer.

Lately, he wondered if he might soon be a victim of divorced parents.

Matt called some friends and told them about Ruth and the lost cat. He asked them if they might be interested in forming a search party. Five friends said they were in, and they would meet at the house to discuss strategy.

The nearby grocery store had visitor maps titled "Parables, Minnesota's Best Kept Secret!" The maps had enough detail to organize a fairly thorough search. After asking permission from the store manager, Matt took seven copies and brought them back to the house.

Shirley smiled as she watched Matt and his friends gather around a large box. Each friend was given a map and assigned an area to search. The two girls in the search party, Melody and Chrissy, asked Matt if he had any extra pictures of Tabby.

"No Chrissy," Matt said, "this is the only one I have."

"That's OK," said Melody. "We'll remember him; he's such a cute cat!"

Matt divided the extra map into six sectors, and each person chose an area to search. His friends wrote down their names and phone numbers in the sector they were covering. They would call in each hour to give updates on what they had found.

Matt picked up the sectioned-off map and was bringing it to his mom when suddenly he stopped. He had another idea.

"Hey, Dad, my friends and I are going to search for the cat that the lady lost. Would it be alright if I gave my friends your phone number, so they could check in? I wrote each person's name and phone number on this map. You could call us and let us know if someone finds him, or if there are any developments."

Shirley watched closely, waiting for Rick's response.

Rick looked up from the box he was unpacking.

"Sorry chief, I just remembered that I have to take care of a few matters." Rick stammered.

With that, he walked out the front door, got into the car, and drove off.

Shirley had to suppress her anger at the bald-faced lie. Matt was disappointed, but not shocked. He had to move on, since his friends were in a hurry, and there were only a few hours of daylight left.

"Matt, give your friends my phone number," Shirley said. "All of you be careful out there, wear your helmets, and I want you to be back here no later than 5:00 pm. That will give you all plenty of time to get home before it gets dark."

"Thanks, Mom," Matt said.

There was disappointment written all over his face as he handed Shirley the master copy. The search party wished each other good luck and prepared to leave. Chrissy walked up to Matt so she could whisper in his ear.

"I'm proud of you Matt!" she said. "This is a nice thing to do."

Matt smiled and blushed slightly. "Thanks for helping Chrissy, and for bringing Melody," he whispered back.

Shirley almost called Rick once the search party left, but she was not ready for another argument.

She decided instead to take a break and meet the neighbor next door.

Perhaps the neighbor had seen Tabby.

CHAPTER 13

Sam Collins sat at his usual table, sipping coffee as he listened to the conversation Lizzy was having with the restaurant owner. She was requesting more shifts and longer hours.

This development concerned Sam.

Lizzy and Sam were close friends. He came to the Creighton Family Restaurant almost every day at the end of the breakfast rush when Lizzy had some time to visit. She would give him updates on her nursing courses, and he would offer her encouragement and support.

Lizzy appreciated Sam's kindness and generosity, and she looked forward to his daily visits. If for some reason he did not show up, she worried. When she mentioned this to Sam, he said he was glad that at least one person in the world cared about him.

For Sam, a retired widower, the restaurant visits were a diversion from the loneliness that filled the greater portion of his days. The loss of his wife, and in recent years the loss of several close friends, took a toll on him. His only son had a busy law practice in Chicago. Sam only saw his son and daughter-in-law during the Christmas season. He barely got to talk to his son, who used the holidays to entertain important clients.

Lizzy had her own struggles. The road to becoming a nurse was difficult. Shortly after high school, her parents were killed in a car accident. They left her with few resources. The few belongings that she inherited had little value. After a long grieving process, Lizzy decided that a nursing career would be a way to honor the memory of her parents.

Lizzy and Sam often confided with each other. Lizzy found Sam to be a compassionate man who listened attentively, and who provided sound advice. Sam deeply admired Lizzy, the hard-charging woman who refused to let any obstacle get in the way of her dream of becoming a nurse.

At the end of each semester, Lizzy shared her grades with Sam. He was honored that she kept him in the loop with her progress. It was a quick review; Lizzy was maintaining a near straight "A" average. But as the courses and clinicals became more intense, Sam noticed the mounting stress was taking a toll on the overextended waitress.

"By golly, Lizzy, you certainly can bring it down a notch!" Sam would often say. "If you got an occasional "B," you're still going to be a great nurse."

Sam knew his words fell on deaf ears. Lizzy was too goal-oriented to let herself slip even slightly. She was focused and determined to do her very best.

Sam thought about the last round of grades that he and Lizzy reviewed together.

"Only one more semester, Lizzy," he said, "and the world will finally enjoy one of the greatest nurses known to mankind."

Lizzy noticed a hint of sadness when Sam said this. He handed back her grades and tried to put on a brave face.

"The only regret I have is that one of those fancy hospitals in a big city will scoop you up, and take you away from here."

Lizzy sat down next to Sam and hugged him.

"Hey, Sammo," she said, "I'm not planning on leaving, and if I do, I'll be sure to make arrangements for you to come too!" Lizzy gave him a quick kiss on the cheek to once again remind him that he was as important to her as she was to him.

So, naturally, the conversation that Sam overheard was confusing. Why would Lizzy ask for more hours when the finish line was just around the bend?

After adjusting her work schedule, Lizzy went over and offered Sam more coffee. When he declined, she looked around and saw that the only other customer was preoccupied with a crossword puzzle. She took a seat across from Sam.

"You look like someone who is burning both ends of the candle, while someone is holding a blow torch to the middle of it!" Sam said in a concerned voice.

Lizzy sighed as she shook her head, trying to wake herself. She then propped her hands under her chin and looked over at Sam with a "wait until you hear my story" look.

"Sam, I'm taking next semester off," Lizzy said.

Sam took a sip of his coffee and set the cup down. He wrapped both hands around the cup and shook his head slightly.

"You mean your LAST semester," Sam said as he looked directly at Lizzy. "There must be a really good reason for that decision. I'm not going to lie. I'm concerned."

Lizzy proceeded to tell Sam about Chance, and the mounting bills. She needed to work the extra hours just to keep up with her monthly expenses.

"I see," said Sam. "Does any of this have to do with your cat that was killed by those boys? What was his name... Max?"

Dear old Sam. Lizzy thought.

He not only was a counselor, supporter, and cheer-leader, he knew the impact major events had on her life.

"Well, yes, in a way Sammo," Lizzy said. "Do you think I'm being foolish here? I know most people would tell me I am, putting a critically injured cat ahead of my career goals."

Sam smiled.

"No, Liz, you're not foolish. If this cat can help you to forgive yourself, then he is a blessing. I know you still blame yourself for Max, and I'm not going to try and convince you for the thousandth time that you were not. If this Chance helps you to feel better, then so be it. But I do have concerns."

"What might those be?" Lizzy asked.

"Lizzy, from what you've told me, this Chance is not out of the woods. And even if he survives, there is no way to tell what impact that entire trauma will have on him. I just hope you've considered all the potential outcomes."

Lizzy assured Sam that she had considered every scenario.

"You know Sam," she said, "If Chance does survive, he will help me to develop patience, understanding, and as you just said, learn to forgive myself and others. I may be taking this semester off, but there will still be lessons learned."

Sam raised his left eyebrow.

"Maybe you need to change his name to Miracle if he can accomplish all that!" Sam said as he reached into his wallet to pay for his coffee. "Do you mind if I go visit this money pit, I mean cat?" Sam asked.

Lizzy smiled and gave Sam the address of the animal hospital.

"Let them know I said it is OK. Wait; let me write a note for you."

Sam watched Lizzy write the note, noticing the sour look on her face.

"Here Sam, if that crazy, mindless receptionist gives you any crap, call me right away."

"Woe, Crazy mindless receptionist?" Sam quipped. "I see Chance hasn't had time yet to work on that patience and understanding you hope to develop!"

Sam walked briskly to the door, while Lizzy followed closely behind. Normally he could escape, but today he was too slow; Lizzy blocked his exit.

"Sam, I can't accept this, it's waaay too much!"

Sam told her to use it for Chance, but Lizzy insisted that he take at least $20 back.

"Look, if you force me to take it, I'm going to use it to buy flowers for the crazy mindless receptionist and say you bought them for her."

Lizzy stuffed the money in her pocket and stomped away.

"*Wow, this receptionist must be a doozy!*" Sam thought.

CHAPTER 14

Shirley admired the warm, inviting porch, tastefully decorated with hanging flower baskets. Two cats were resting on top of the sofa near the window. They gazed at her as she climbed the steps. She rang the bell and smiled when an older woman partially opened the door.

"Hello, I'm Shirley Carver, your new neighbor!" Shirley said while extending her hand.

Grace Peterson kept the door partially opened, refusing to acknowledge Shirley's gesture of friendship.

"What do you want?" she asked tersely.

Shirley was thrown off by the cold reception.

"Well, I came to say hello, and get acquainted…"

Grace did not indicate that she was interested.

Shirley was disappointed with the reception. She decided to get to the other reason for her visit and then get back to unpacking.

"Also, I believe you know Ruth, the former owner of the house, right?"

Grace nodded.

"She came by our house today, and she was extremely upset. Her cat escaped when she was moving into her new apartment in Newton Bay. She is holding out hope that somehow, he made his way back to his old home. My son

Matt and his friends are out looking for him now. I was wondering if you might have seen him." Shirley stammered.

"Newton Bay!" Grace exclaimed. "That's over 28 miles from here!"

"I know it's a long shot, but…"

"I thought that was Tabby." Grace interrupted, as her head slumped.

"Oh, so you have seen him!' Shirley replied.

Grace raised her head, and Shirley now saw the tears.

"I'm so sorry, did something happen to Tabby?" Shirley asked.

"DID SOMETHING HAPPEN?!" Grace yelled.

Grace flung open the door and flew into a fit of anger.

"Yes, something happened to Tabby!" Grace blurted. "The other day I was headed over to your house to greet your husband, who had just pulled into the driveway. I made some freshly baked zucchini bread; it was still warm. I stopped when I noticed your husband was staggering and thought it would be better to come back another time. But as I turned to leave, I saw a cat, sitting near the door, wet, muddy, injured, and obviously in distress."

Grace pulled out a tissue from the pocket of her sweater, wiped her eyes, and then continued.

"My eyesight ain't what it used to be," Grace said, "but I thought it might be Tabby. I started to walk toward the house and see for sure, and that's when it happened…"

"What happened?" Shirley asked, bracing for the answer.

Grace was shaking, trying to calm herself so she could continue. When Shirley tried to hold her arm, Grace pulled away.

"That, that beast, your husband, yelled at Tabby to move away from the door. When Tabby did not move, your husband went up to him, and kicked him as hard as he could!! Tabby went flying; I've never in my life heard an animal screech like that! Tabby's leg was surely broken…he tried to run but the leg kept giving out on him. I watched as he hid under some nearby bushes. I wanted to go and rescue him, but your husband…."

Shirley felt sick. This couldn't be happening. She wanted to be enjoying a cup of tea with Grace, enjoying a piece of her zucchini bread, getting acquainted, and beginning a new friendship.

"That's not the worst of it!" Grace scowled.

Shirley did not want to hear more but knew she needed to hear the whole story.

"I hoped your husband would leave so I could get to Tabby. I thought I would have my chance when he staggered out of the house and headed toward his car. But he saw Tabby hiding under the bushes. My God, before I knew it, he went into the house and came out with a broom. He charged at Tabby, yelling, and when that poor cat tried to run on that broken leg, he hit him hard! I could see Tabby bleeding. That menace tried to hit him again, but he was so drunk that he fell backward. Tabby, he somehow got up, and limped…."

Grace had to pause; the memory of the scene was too much. After a few moments, she continued.

"That poor cat struggled to get back here from Newton Bay, only to be beaten and killed by your husband…that poor cat never hurt anyone! You and your husband, just stay away from me!!"

With that, Grace went back into her house and slammed the door.

Shirley's head was throbbing as she left her traumatized neighbor. The cats continued to watch her from the sofa.

Her phone rang several times. Matt and his friends reported what areas could be crossed off the map, as they continued their futile search for a missing cat killed by Rick.

Shirley entered the house, went into the closet, and retrieved the broom. Blood and fur were still trapped in the bristles.

Shirley repacked some clothes for herself and Matt. She would tell Rick that his heartless deed was observed by a neighbor. She would present the broom as evidence, knowing that Rick would vehemently deny all allegations. Once the suitcase was packed, she made a call.

"Hi Dad, it's Shirley. Would you be able to come to the house? Matt and I need to stay with you and Mom for a while if that's OK."

Her dad asked for no explanation. "I'll be there in an hour."

****

Rick was ordered to leave the Honeybee Lounge, or wait for the police. He was sober enough to know that he'd better leave. After a few harsh words, he staggered to his car and drove home.

Shirley was waiting for him as he parked the car in the driveway. He almost tripped as he exited the car. He took a moment to regain his balance and composure, and then walked as steadily as he could toward the porch.

Shirley just stared at Rick, watching as he struggled to feign sobriety.

"Honey, I'm sorry. My head is killing me." Rick said. "I need to lie down and get some rest. I promise I will help once I feel better."

Shirley followed him into the house, not saying a word. Rick paused a moment, waited for a response, then turned and headed for the bedroom.

"Were you drunk when you did it?" Shirley suddenly asked.

Rick stopped and turned around. "Did what?" he snarled.

Shirley took a deep breath, so she could remain calm.

"When you kicked the cat and broke his leg. When you beat him with our broom and then forced him to flee, so he could die a slow, painful death?"

Rick whipped around and returned Shirley's stare with a scowl. "What the hell are you talking about!?"

"I went to meet our new neighbor, hoping to get acquainted. It turns out she knew the lost cat."

"Wonderful!" Rick snarled with as much sarcasm as he could muster. "What does this have to do with anything?"

"Everything!!" Shirley yelled back. "Our neighbor was stopping by the other day to welcome us when you provided her with a horror show! You viciously kicked the lost cat, whose name is Tabby, in case you forgot. You broke his leg and likely caused other serious injuries. But you weren't done! You decided to finish the job! You got one of the few things you unpacked, a broom, and hit him with it. You went to hit him again, but fell backward because as usual, you were drunk!"

Shirley paused, to make sure Rick was getting the full picture.

"Why am I such a fool? Why did I think you could change?" Shirley asked.

After pausing again, Shirley continued.

"You lied to Ruth, telling her you hadn't seen her cat!" Shirley yelled. "That poor, lost, injured cat was only trying to find its owner, and instead he found a monster! Matt and his friends are still out looking for a cat that you butchered. And you terrified our neighbor, an elderly lady!"

Rick had enough.

"Shut up!!!" Rick yelled. "That old bat doesn't know what she's talking about! I never saw the cat!"

Shirley grabbed the broom and showed Rick the bloodstains and bits of fur.

"You liar!" Shirley yelled as she started to cry. "You're nothing but a violent, lying drunk!"

Rick threw the broom to the side and grabbed Shirley's arm. The accumulated alcohol in his system fired up his anger to an uncontrolled level.

"I told you to shut up!" Rick yelled.

When Shirley started to speak again, he raised his free hand.

Matt and his friends came through the door, just as Rick clenched his fist and struck Shirley's face, causing her nose to bleed.

Matt dropped his map and ran to push Rick away from Shirley.

"Leave her alone!" Matt yelled, while his friends looked on.

Rick froze and then took in the scene before him. He staggered out the door, climbed into the car, and sped away.

Matt ran to search for the first aid kit. His friends were stunned and quietly left the house. Grace heard the commotion and watched Rick's exit. After a few minutes, she saw Melody and Chrissy emerge from the house, visibly upset as they prepared to ride their bikes home.

"Girls, wait," Grace called. "What just happened?"

"Matt's dad hit his mom, and made her nose bleed!" Melody said while shaking.

"Melody, be quiet!" Chrissy whispered.

Grace bowed her head, feeling scared and responsible at the same time. Trembling, she went into her house, and for the first time in over 20 years, she closed the door ...

and locked it.

CHAPTER 15

Marge looked up from her work to see a neatly dressed man approaching her desk. Sam Collins introduced himself, as Marge smiled while attempting to straighten her hair, a habit she did when she was nervous or intimidated.

"*She seems nice enough.*" Sam thought to himself.

"And how may I help you?" Marge asked.

Something about Sam's appearance, his polite introduction, and that smile brought back a feeling that Marge had not felt in years. She felt herself blush.

"*Shame on you, Marge Sutter!*" she thought to herself.

"I'm here to see a friend's cat," Sam replied.

Marge's smile was replaced by a look of disappointment. There were only a few cats in the hospital; most were there for the day.

Only one needed a visitor.

"Name?" asked Marge, trying to disguise the fact she already knew.

"Lizzy Candone," Sam replied. "She gave me this authorization to visit her cat, Chance."

He reached into his pocket and handed it to Marge. He watched as Marge read it, and tried not to smile as Marge's face reacted to Lizzy's sarcasm:

To Whom It May Concern:

I am authorizing Sam Collins to visit my Cat, which I named "Chance" (please update your files if you have not already done so). Mr. Collins should be treated nicely, and not judged as someone who would shoot a giraffe at the zoo while little children are feeding it marshmallows. He is a kind, considerate man, and loves animals. If you need further authorization, please call me immediately (i.e. right away). Please remember that a good portion of the costs I am incurring for Chance's treatment is going toward your salary.

Sincerely,

"Lizzy" Condone (pronounced "Can-Done," where the "e" is silent and not a separate syllable, and "Done" rhymes with "Own." Sam can walk you through it a few times if this challenges your verbal skills)

Marge sighed as she folded the note.

"I'll be right back; I have to check to see if the cat is in his cage, and also let the doctor know."

Susan chuckled as she read Lizzy's note; then she quickly apologized to Marge. Susan followed Marge to her desk.

"Hello, I'm Susan McNamara, the Veterinarian who is tending to Chance," Susan said, as she extended her hand to greet Sam. "I'd like to go over his case with you if you have time Mr. Collins. I want you to be prepared before you go in to see Chance."

Sam nodded, as Susan led him to her office.

Susan gave Sam a thorough history of Chance's treatment and made it clear that he was still in very bad shape. After she was certain Sam understood the situation, she asked about his relationship with Lizzy.

Sam rubbed his chin. "I'm wondering if that nice-looking lady...Marge I believe, would also like to hear the story?"

Susan peeked out of her office. "Marge, could you come into my office, and close the door behind you?"

Marge put the "Ring Bell for Service" sign up, and went into Susan's office, a look of dismay on her face.

Sam smiled as Marge took a seat. He thanked her for coming into the office and explained that he thought she should hear more about Lizzy.

Susan noticed Marge was listening intently as Sam recounted his relationship with Lizzy. She seemed as interested in Sam as she was in his story.

"We look out for each other," Sam said. "Things were moving along nicely. Lizzy was keeping her grades up, even while working at the restaurant. And then those boys went and killed her cat."

Marge felt a lump forming in her throat.

"I met Max a few times." Sam continued. "He was a nice cat, and he sure loved Lizzy. He was her night ranger, always waiting for her to arrive home after a long day of work and school."

As Sam talked about the demise of Max, Marge could only look down at the floor and shake her head.

"I recall that whole incident," Susan said. "A lot of people still feel the boys got off too easy. Judge Logan took some heat, but he hoped that by meeting the victims the boys would experience first-hand the emotional toll of their cruel acts. The judge got through to at least one of them. He comes here regularly to volunteer. At first, I was reluctant to have him around the hospital, given his history. But his therapist asked me to use him on a trial basis. He works hard and is great with the animals. He has changed, but perhaps I should make sure he is not working when Lizzy comes by."

"That might be best for now," Sam said. "I keep hoping that she has moved on. But now I'm not so sure."

Marge finally looked up. "I had no idea, I honestly didn't," she told Sam. "You see, when she came in that night with Chance, I jumped to the conclusion that the fox story was used as an excuse. There is no way a fox would have done all that damage. A fox generally will not even tangle with a cat. I've seen so many abused animals lately...I see now why Lizzy reacted the way she did. I'm such a fool, I should have..."

Sam took her hand and cut her off.

"There is no way you could have known what happened to Max. As you've seen, Lizzy is passionate, often to a fault! Give it a little time; she will get over it; she has to. She realizes that as a nurse, she will need to keep her emotions in check if she is to succeed."

Susan got up and took Sam back to see Chance, while Marge returned to her desk. Chance was sleeping, breathing heavily.

"I'm honestly amazed he's made it this far." Susan confided. "His appetite has improved slightly. I'm still not getting my hopes up."

"My goodness, it's heartbreaking to see what some animals have to suffer," Sam said while shaking his head. "I won't get my hopes up either. But Lizzy is set on giving him a chance...hence the name selection."

Susan smiled.

After leaving Chance, Sam asked Susan if he could discuss one more matter.

"I understand that the costs are mounting for Chance's care," Sam said with a concerned look. "Lizzy decided to put nursing school on hold so she could work longer hours and pay the costs, and I just can't let that happen. Not when she is so close to finishing."

"I understand what you're saying, Mr. Collins, but I have a business to run, and…"

"Please, call me Sam."

"Ok, Sam. I have a lot of financial pressures myself, and…"

"No, you're getting the wrong idea, can I call you Susan?" Sam asked.

"Yes."

"I want to pay the bills," Sam said. "Lizzy is too close to finishing. She has classes and clinicals already lined up. If she stops now, there's a possibility she may never go back. I can't risk that."

"I see," Susan said. "Well, you are a very generous man Sam. I will admit that I'm relieved too; I would feel guilty asking for payments knowing now that Lizzy is so close to graduating. You can make the arrangements with Marge."

Sam pulled out his checkbook and met with Marge to pay the current balance. He arranged to cover additional amounts as they accrued.

"And what should I tell Lizzy?" Marge asked.

"I'm still working on that," Sam said. "For now, just don't request any more payments."

Marge nodded as she updated the system to include Sam's information. Sam smiled at Marge and started to say something else. But then he paused and turned toward the door.

"Feel free to come back," Marge said. "I will keep Lizzy's authorization on file, so you have permission to see Chance any time during our regular work hours."

Marge blushed, as she realized what she said sounded like an invitation.

Sam smiled again, stopped, and went back to Marge's desk.

"Say, I know we just met, and if I'm being a little too forward, just say so. But I was wondering if you would like to go out for coffee or dinner? Not at Lizzy's restaurant, of course."

Marge now was in full blush mode; Sam pretended not to notice.

"Yes, I would like that." she blurted.

"There's a new Italian restaurant near here," Sam said. "I could meet you tomorrow after you're done working if that's not too soon."

Marge said that would be fine. The few customers in the waiting area who were pretending to be busy on their cell phones could not help but smile when Marge said yes.

Susan also heard their interaction from her office and also smiled.

"What an intriguing development." she thought.

CHAPTER 16

Ruth was rotating between rounds of restless sleep and long episodes of insomnia. Her energy nearly depleted, she wondered how she could return to work in a week. The grieving process continued its rugged journey, and she had no one to navigate it with.

The phone rang. It was her mom.

"Hi, Mom."

"Hello Honey." Ruth's mom said, trying to hide the concern in her voice. "Would it be alright if your father and I came over, and helped you get settled in? We could stay over if you like, keep you company, or we could stay at a hotel if…"

"Sure Mom, I'd like that, if it's not too much trouble," Ruth said.

She could hear her mom sigh, obviously relieved that Ruth accepted the offer. Ruth gave her father directions, and he said they would be there soon.

Grateful for some company, Ruth took the opportunity to use the brief mood boost for a walk, in hopes of clearing her mind. Everywhere she walked, there were reward posters. Tony had saturated the town. If the fires of revenge were still burning, Ruth would have paid some teenagers to call Tony with false sightings of Tabby, thus sending him on one wild goose chase after another, only to have his hopes dashed each time.

The fires of revenge were rapidly dying out; she had no desire to rekindle them.

****

Tony was driving to Newton Bay twice a day; early in the morning and in the evening after work. The 56-mile round trips along with the fruitless searches were not only time-consuming but also created new rounds of tension with Olivia.

"There are posters all over that town Tony, I don't want you to go back there!" she demanded.

Tony knew Olivia needed a break from all of the stress of the last few months, so he reluctantly agreed. What Olivia wanted was for Tony to move on and accept that Tabby was gone. There was a lot to do to prepare for the baby, who was due in a few short weeks. The lost cat put everything on hold.

Tony resorted to texting Ruth since there were no responses to his posters. Ruth ignored his requests to leave food out, to check on the posters, and to see if any of her neighbors had seen Tabby. The texts went unanswered; until Ruth finally sent a reply that made it clear that Tony needed to stop.

"Does Olivia know you're texting me?"

Tony discontinued the texts.

****

The walk did not do much to improve Ruth's mood. The posters, each still holding a complete set of tabs, increased the guilt she felt. The tabs made a snapping noise when a strong gust of wind passed through them as if beckoning for her attention. Ruth knew the good people of

Newton Bay who read the posters would be concerned; some might have even engaged in a pointless search.

Ruth's parents arrived to find their daughter looking awful and the apartment in total disarray. After long hugs and no questions, Ruth's mom encouraged her to lie down and try to get some rest, while they did some unpacking and organizing.

For the first time in weeks, Ruth fell into a sound sleep.

She woke up five hours later to total darkness; the smell of a home-cooked dinner permeated the air. Her parents were talking softly as they worked on the apartment. Ruth opened the door to the bedroom, and could not believe the progress her parents had made.

"Mom, Dad, I'm so sorry! You should have woken me up so I could help you."

"Perfect timing Ruth, dinner is almost ready!" her mom said. "I had to start it late since it took a little time to find and unpack your kitchen items. If you'd like to freshen up, go ahead. It will be ready in about 20 - 25 minutes."

"*Freshen up*." Ruth thought. Yes, her hygiene had slipped badly.

"I might take a quick shower if that's OK Mom?"

"Definitely!" Ruth's mom replied. "Your father found those comfy pajamas we bought you for your birthday if you'd like to put those on so you can relax."

Before Ruth could reply, her dad scurried over and handed her the flannel pajamas.

"Thanks, Dad!" Ruth said, as her father smiled nervously.

The shower was a perfect tonic, along with the arrival of her parents. They had suffered with her throughout the divorce, and they were not about to abandon her now.

Ruth came into the kitchen wearing the pajamas and took a seat. Her mom had cooked her favorite dinner, eggplant parmesan with pasta and homemade marinara sauce. The dinner was planned. After her father said the blessing, Ruth ate as much as she could. Her appetite was still waning, but she forced herself to indulge in the carefully cooked meal.

"Honey," Ruth's mom eventually said, "We found out about Tabby."

Ruth froze as her dad took out one of Tony's posters from his shirt pocket.

"What happened?" her dad asked. "And why does that meathead have his phone number on the poster!?! The judge gave Tabby to you!"

Ruth's mom told him to calm down. She then told Ruth that her father drove around town for an hour in the hope of finding Tabby, but he had no success.

Ruth felt the sick feeling come over her again, as she wondered what to tell her parents.

Should she think of another carefully crafted lie?

CHAPTER 17

"Please Dad, can we discuss it later?" Shirley begged.

Shirley's dad wanted answers. The napkin Shirley applied to her nose was saturated with blood. The bleeding periodically stopped when she held her head back. She took a direct hit, and the areas under her eyes were already turning black. Questions would be asked and reports filled out at the hospital. Eventually, Shirley would need to recount what happened, but it was clear that she did not want to discuss it now. Shirley insisted that they go to a hospital 45 miles from Parables. She did not want to risk running into friends or acquaintances. The fact that Matt and his friends witnessed what happened was horrible enough.

Her dad drove on in silence, gripping the steering wheel. He knew something like this might happen one day. And now that it did, his mind was racing in numerous directions.

As the rain trickled down the windows, Matt stared out at the passing terrain from the back seat. His young mind wrestled with a myriad of emotions; anger, despair, embarrassment, and loneliness. As he had done so many times before, Matt tried to think of what went wrong, and what he should have done to keep it from happening.

Shirley's father broke the gloomy silence.

"Honey, your face is starting to swell," he said, "I'm going to make a quick stop, and get some ice and gauze pads. Your mom is bringing some fresh clothes to the hospital. We may have a wait in the ER, and that napkin needs to be replaced. Do you want me to get any pain medication?"

Shirley nodded.

They pulled into a mini-mart; Shirley's dad rushed in, almost crashing into a young couple who were exiting. The man swore at him, as the girl pulled him away and into their car. Shirley was glad it went no further. Her father was retired and did not deserve to be in this situation.

"I hate him, Mom!!" Matt suddenly yelled, his voice quivering. Tears of a hundred broken dreams and empty promises flowed.

"He's a liar, he's a killer, and he's a coward!" Matt wailed.

He no longer tried to make excuses for Rick. There were none.

"I understand how you feel, Matt," Shirley said quietly.

"I hate what he did to you Mom. My friends saw everything! He hurt you, he killed that cat! He promises me everything, but all I ever get from him is disappointment...."

Matt's fists and teeth were clenched as he returned to gazing out the window.

Shirley's dad scrambled back into the car. After helping Shirley, he continued driving to the hospital. His mind shifted to the legal issues ahead; hiring a lawyer, obtaining a restraining order, filing for divorce and custody for Matt, selling the house they had just bought, and all the other little details that his daughter would need to take care of in the weeks, months and years ahead. He would need to write things down so that when Shirley was ready to talk, he could help her through the process.

The metric thumping of the windshield wipers once again was the only sound inside the car. They arrived at the hospital, and Shirley's mom gasped as she took her first look at her daughter. Matt went with his grandfather to park the car. The Emergency Room was packed; the wait for non-life-threatening situations would be at least an hour, if not more. Matt went with his grandfather to the cafeteria, and after getting some frozen yogurt, they sat in a quiet corner.

"Thanks for coming to get us, Grandpa," Matt said somberly.

"No need to thank me, Matt. I'm sorry you have to go through all of this. How are you doing?"

Matt looked at his grandfather, his eyes were red and swollen.

"I'll be OK, I guess," he said. "I don't understand why he does it. I think he wants to change, but then he can't. He can't stop drinking. He makes promises and then breaks them. I can't get my hopes up anymore Grandpa. It hurts too much. And I don't think I can ever forgive him for what he did to mom. Is that wrong to feel that way? Am I breaking a commandment?"

"No Matt, it's your dad who is breaking commandments; a lot of them. You and your mom will have to stay with us, at least until we get some things figured out. If you need to talk to me, I'm always available. There are also other people you can talk to if you're not comfortable just talking to me."

Matt nodded. He dipped his spoon into the frozen yogurt, as he and his grandfather struggled to swallow a treat that they always enjoyed together.

"*How sad Matt got stuck with Rick as his father.*" Shirley's dad thought. He knew he had to be careful about what he said to Matt; "hold his tongue" as the saying went. He would try as much as possible to give Matt and Shirley the space they needed.

****

Shirley's name was eventually called, and her mom accompanied her into the room. The staff started their examination. They had seen it all: beatings, stabbings, gunshot wounds, and broken bones.

A nurse took down Shirley's information, checked her blood pressure, and gently removed the gauze that was sticking to her drying blood.

"May I ask how this happened?" the nurse asked.

"My husband assaulted me," Shirley said calmly.

The nurse nodded. "Were they any witnesses?" she asked.

"My son and his friends saw the whole thing."

"We need to report this to the police." the nurse said after a short pause.

"Please do," Shirley responded.

Rick had to be stopped. He had crossed the line. He came close before, and now it happened. Rick was an abuser. He abused her. He abused Matt. He abused animals. And above all, Rick abused himself. He refused to get help, so she needed to protect herself and Matt.

"Do you have somewhere safe to stay?" The nurse asked.

Shirley's mom said she did.

The nurse finished and then left the room. Shortly after, a doctor entered and reviewed the information. He cleaned the area and then did his examination. The force of the blow had indeed broken her nose. The doctor did a realignment and then packed it. When he was all finished, Shirley looked like a car wreck survivor. She was given a prescription for pain medicine and told to limit her activities for at least two weeks.

The state police arrived and filed a report, and asked if they could take some photos to support an arrest warrant for Rick. Shirley obliged. After filling the prescriptions, they went to Shirley's parent's home.

Matt had just gone to bed when his phone rang.

It was Chrissy.

"Hi," Matt said somberly, as he answered the phone.

"Hi," Chrissy replied. "Are you OK?"

Her whispering told Matt that Chrissy was calling in secret. Matt said he was, though his voice told a different story.

"Does everyone know what happened?" Matt asked.

Chrissy paused, wondering how to reply. Finally, she opened up.

"The police just came here and asked me what I saw. I'm sure they went to talk to the others too. So, our parents know. I didn't tell anyone, Matt! My parents were upset that I didn't say anything to them. My dad said I can't go back to your house."

I'm sorry Chrissy." Matt said.

"Don't say that!" Chrissy retorted. "You didn't do anything wrong!"

Chrissy heard her mom approaching.

"I have to go. I'll call you when I can."

Matt said OK.

"I miss you, Matt!" Chrissy confided as she ended the call.

Matt reconnected the phone to his charger. He hoped Chrissy erased the call history, or her parents might take away her phone. He missed her too. Chrissy and his other friends might never be part of his life again. And even if they were, it wouldn't be the same.

The mounting losses crushed the young boy's spirit. He took out the picture of Rick that he kept in his wallet. He tore it up until the pieces were too small to rip any further. Then he gathered them up and threw them out.

As far as he was concerned, he no longer had a father.

CHAPTER 18

Marge wanted to go "Dutch treat" when the dinner bill arrived, but Sam said he was not Dutch. The food was good, and the conversation, though awkward at first, soon flowed easily. They talked about their lives, their families, and even their deceased spouses. Sam talked about his son and Marge about her two sons.

"What is it about sons?" Marge asked Sam. "I know they love me, but they get so busy with their work. I feel like when I call them, I am being a nuisance. Fortunately, they have wonderful wives, and I spend a lot of time talking to them. And they are my best allies when it comes to getting my sons to keep in touch with me."

"I have to take a lot of the blame for my relationship with my son," Sam said. "Harry Chapin could have written "Cats in the Cradle" based on my fathering skills. I was too busy when my son came along, and my wife was always trying to get me to spend more time with him. When she was dying, she begged me to strengthen our relationship. But in a lot of ways, it was too late. I missed the boat. And now, he's grown and much too busy for me."

"Sam," Marge said, "it's never too late. I've begun to remind my boys that their father is gone, and someday so will I. Now that they are parents, they realize the love I have for them is the same as the love they have for their children. In the last few years, our relationships have slowly gotten stronger."

"I hope so," Sam said. "My daughter-in-law is pregnant, and I want to be part of my grandchild's life. I'm hoping the baby will be a bridge to working things out."

"Well, if not, at least you have Lizzy," Marge said.

Sam sighed and shook his head.

"To be honest Marge, once Lizzy is done with school and is a full-time nurse, she won't need me much. I know she loves me, and I think of her as the daughter I never had. But things will change; life moves on. She won't be pouring me coffee at the restaurant as we have our daily chats. She'll get married to Ben, and her life will take off, just as it should. We will always be a part of one another's lives, but it will be … different."

Marge nodded.

"So enough about me; your turn," Sam said. "How did you end up working at the animal hospital?"

"Well, it's not too complicated," Marge said. "There was an ad in the *Parables News* for an opening as the receptionist. I'm a retired bookkeeper, and I needed something to do after my husband died. I love animals, so it looked like a good fit."

"That Susan sure seems to be an excellent veterinarian," Sam said. "The job she performed on that poor cat is incredible."

"She is an excellent vet, but she's a horrible business person. When I started, the place was in survival mode. She worked late each night, trying to catch up with the administrative work. I heard a lot of customers requesting lower fees. Some even wanted her to do a service for free!" Marge said in an exasperated voice while rolling her eyes.

"I asked to meet with her one evening after the hospital closed." Marge continued. "I told her my background and asked If I could help her out. She was genuinely grateful. Well, I took care of the billing and made sure payments were timely, and for the full amounts. I took care of payroll and other accounting tasks. Susan was able to spend her time on what she was destined to be: one of the best veterinarians in the state."

"She's lucky you came along," Sam said as he took a sip of his coffee. "Has she given you a bonus?"

"Sam, I would never accept a bonus from her!" Marge objected. "She is like a daughter to me. She tells me to give myself a raise, and I thank her. Since I do the payroll, she has no clue that I never give myself a raise. If I could get away with it, I would work for free."

Sam smiled. "Well, it looks like we have a lot in common."

Marge returned Sam's smile.

"So, what is the hardest part of your job?" Sam asked.

"It's the abused animals that come in," Marge said, "and the ones that are abandoned. It used to be a rarity in Parables, but it's becoming more common. I don't like it. It doesn't sit well with me."

"I hear you," Sam said. "The more this town grows, the farther it drifts from the values that made it such a great place. I don't know what to make of it."

They finished dinner and had their leftovers packed up. After Sam paid the bill, they stopped for ice cream at a shop nearby. Marge treated.

"Sam, I had a wonderful evening," Marge said as they arrived at the veterinarian hospital.

"I did too Marge." Sam replied, "Can we do this again?"

Marge hugged Sam and smiled.

"You know where to find me."

CHAPTER 19

Ruth asked her parents to sit down, as she tried to get her thoughts together. Despite the 5-hour nap, she was still tired. Now, she was also tired of lying. She decided to tell her parents everything. Would they understand? Her parents loved Tabby. What would they think of her when they heard the truth?

As Ruth detailed the events of Tabby's demise, her parents listened quietly. They realized that Ruth's wounds were deeper than they imagined. Had Ruth allowed herself time to process her pain, harming Tabby would never have been an option.

But what was done was done.

Ruth's father put on his jacket and was heading for the door to look for Tabby.

"Dad, it's too late!' Ruth wailed. "He's been gone too long. I don't even remember where I left him. He has no chip, no collar, and no means of identification. He likely did not survive the night. If a car or truck didn't kill him, then a coyote likely did. I just hope he didn't suffer."

Ruth's parents realized she was right. Tabby could not have survived this long. Tony's posters were useless. Additional search efforts were all but a waste of time.

"Honey," Ruth's mom sighed, "I'm so sorry. Would it be alright if I stay with you for a few days, give you some time to settle in? You need help to deal with everything that's happened. All this turmoil in your life, the betrayal, the divorce, the move to a new town, and now Tabby; it's a heavy toll."

"Yes, I would like that," Ruth said as she melted into her mom's arms.

Her father gently rubbed her shoulders, desperately wondering what he could do to help fix his little girl. Eventually, Ruth composed herself and embraced her parents.

"I'm so glad you both are here. I don't know how to deal with all of this," she said.

The tone of her voice revealed a defeated spirit.

"I never should have fought for Tabby," Ruth said. "He deserved to be with Tony; it was his mom's cat. Tabby would have been happy with them, and their baby would have loved him, and...."

"Enough." Her father whispered as he held Ruth's hands. "Remember, 'Mr. Wonderful' hurt you in the worst way possible. As far as I'm concerned, Tabby's on his head. He never thought about anyone but himself. Now he will have a little lesson about hurt. I hope he keeps up his futile search; he deserves to get his chain yanked!"

Ruth smiled as she recalled her father's reaction when he found out about Tony's infidelity. Despite his age, he challenged Tony to a fist fight in the parking lot where Tony worked. A security guard came and escorted her father off of the property.

Tony made every effort to avoid Ruth's parents from that point forward.

"Come into the kitchen, let's finish eating." Ruth's mom said.

Ruth ate a bit more. Having her parents with her allowed her to regain a slight appetite. Afterward, Ruth rehashed the incident with Tabby in greater detail, from the early days of planning to the actual execution. Over and over again, she said she would do anything to go back and stop herself. She told her parents about her disrupted sleep and the worsening depression.

Her parents let her talk, hoping it released some of the pain she was holding inside. After dinner, her father went out and brought in a fully packed suitcase for her mom.

"I was hoping you would say I could stay," Ruth's mom said with a smile, "So, I came prepared."

Her father put on his jacket as he prepared to leave. He had to work the next day, so it would be better if he went home. After giving both his wife and Ruth a kiss, he said he would still do a little searching for Tabby while there was some daylight.

"I'll call if I have any luck," he said.

"Just be careful Dad, and remember to leave your blinkers on if you park on the side of the road. And if a police officer happens to stop and asks what you are doing, don't tell him you had to pee."

Her father's eyes widened.

"What?" he asked.

"Never mind," Ruth said.

CHAPTER 20

Sam sat in his usual booth, waiting for Lizzy to take his order. She was walking toward him, carrying two carafes of coffee; one regular, one decaf. She smiled as she approached Sam, holding the carafes in the air.

"The usual combo Sam, half and half?"

Sam covered his mug before she started pouring.

"Better make it three-quarters decaf, and one-quarter regular," Sam replied. "I seem to sleep better if I don't have too much octane in the bloodstream when nighttime rolls around."

Lizzy poured the requested combination, set the carafes back at the coffee station, and came back to visit with Sam. Lizzy was anxious to hear Sam's assessment.

"So, what did you think of Chance? I mean I know he is still in bad shape, but I think he's a fighter. I'm hoping that somehow he pulls through."

"Well, Liz, you're right, he is a fighter. I can't believe he survived with everything he's been through. That vet Susan is amazed that he's held on this long. She's never seen a case like Chance. I think she is cautiously optimistic."

Lizzy smiled at the positive news.

"Well," Lizzy said with a sigh, "I have to make another visit tomorrow to pay the piper. I also need to withdraw from my classes. The school only gives full refunds if there is an emergency. Do you think I'd be lying if I said a close relative was in a terrible accident and needs my care?" Lizzy asked as she turned around to make sure no customers were waiting.

"I got some good news on that end too," Sam said while he rubbed his chin. "There are grants available for abused animals that need extensive care. Chance qualifies, so his expenses have been paid, and will continue to be paid until he recovers."

Lizzy spun around and tried to make eye contact with Sam, who was trying to avoid making eye contact with her. Lizzy read right through Sam's story. She knew him too well.

"Wow, that's great!" Lizzy said. "What was the name of the organization that provided the funds?"

"Ah, I can't remember offhand," Sam said, still rubbing his chin.

"I see. I'll just call that excuse for a receptionist and see if she can give me the information. I need to call them immediately and thank them!"

Lizzy pulled out her phone, and Sam realized he was busted.

"Ok little Miss Smarty Pants, the name of the organization is called SWOILFS!" Sam said, looking a bit annoyed.

Lizzy laughed. "The what?" she asked.

"SWOILFS," Sam repeated.

He took a napkin, and wrote "Sam's – Way – of – Insuring – Lizzy – Finishes - School."

Lizzy read the napkin and laughed again. Sam was at his best when she backed him into a corner.

"Sam," she said, "I can't take your money. Chance is my responsibility. I'm the one who decided to try and save him, and…"

"Stop!" Sam interrupted, trying to not raise his voice too much. "You're too close Lizzy, the finish line is in view. You have momentum, and it's irresponsible for you to stop now. Consider it an early graduation present…"

"Sam, I can't. You've already been too generous with me over the years. I appreciate your concern, but I can't accept it! I just…"

Lizzy stopped when a teardrop hit her hand.

"I've been generous to you?" Sam said as he wiped his eyes. "Lizzy, don't you realize how generous you've been to me? Sometimes, no, most of the time, the best part of my week is coming here to talk to you. That may sound a bit crazy, seeing as some days you only have a few minutes. But even then, the time you take to talk to me, well, it carries me."

Lizzy looked at Sam as he kept wiping his eyes.

"Sam, look, you have been too generous with me for as long as I've known you. I just can't let you spend your money on a cat that I chose to rescue. It wouldn't be right."

"Not right?" Sam rebutted. "What would be right? Do you think I have some mile-long bucket list to work on? Do you think I am neglecting myself? I have everything I need or want! Don't deprive me of this Lizzy! I thought by now you realized that you're my family. My world is shrinking fast, and you need to realize how important this is to me! You…"

Sam trailed off; he was too choked up to continue.

Lizzy realized that there was no choice in the matter. To turn Sam down would be to hurt him, plain and simple. He was invested in seeing her graduate more than she realized. If Sam was right, and he usually was, it was dangerous for her to pull out of school at this juncture. There would be no guarantees that her financial situation would improve the next semester. She would miss clinicals and the valuable experience she was getting at the local hospital.

"Alright, you win Sammo," Lizzy said. "But when I graduate and get a position, I will pay you back."

Sam nodded, even though he had no intention of letting her pay him back. That battle could wait.

"Sam, I know I've told you before, but I couldn't have made this journey without you," Lizzy said as she took his hands. "Every time I felt overwhelmed, or was ready to give up, I could count on you to encourage me, to stop the negative thoughts, and get me to believe in myself. I love to see the excitement in your eyes when I share my grades with you. I always knew that when you told me you are proud of me, you meant it."

An older couple was waiting to be served. Lizzy got up and gave Sam a hug and a kiss on the forehead.

"Thanks, Sammo. We'll talk later."

Sam nodded as he got up and headed toward the door.

The older man was smiling as Lizzy arrived at the table.

"Do all of your customers get a hug and a kiss?" he asked.

The man grimaced when his wife kicked him in the shin from across the table.

"Well, your wife has to sign a waiver," Lizzy replied. "And you have to meet the minimum order and tip requirement."

At the end of their meal, the wife ordered her husband to triple the tip. Lizzy tried to reduce it, saying she was just joking, but the wife insisted.

"Well now, I guess I made the tip requirement," the man said with a grin.

Lizzy nodded and waited for permission.

"Just be careful," the wife said with a wink, "the old coot has a heart condition."

Lizzy hugged the man and walked away.

"Hey!" He protested. "What about the kiss?"

"Sorry, can't take the chance. Our AED is in the shop." Lizzy said.

The man gave his wife a look of contempt for ratting about his heart. Suddenly Lizzy wrapped her arms around him from behind and delivered a peck on his cheek. He chuckled as he rose from the booth and put on his jacket.

"We may be back tomorrow for breakfast, lunch and dinner!" he told Lizzy as they headed for the door.

"Could you make it for Friday?" Lizzy asked.

"Why, are you not working until then?"

"No, our AED will be back on Friday," Lizzy said.

The wife gave Lizzy the thumbs up.

"Thanks!" she said. "I think a good laugh is as good or better for him as all the medications he is on."

"That's what they tell us in nursing school," Lizzy replied.

"You are going to make a great nurse!" she said as she clasped both of Lizzy's hands.

"Thanks, I appreciate that," Lizzy said. "It's been a long road, and I seem to still doubt myself as I get closer to the finish."

"Well dear, I will add you to my prayer list, asking that you have confidence and peace of mind. Keep your head up!"

"Thanks, I will!" Lizzy said.

CHAPTER 21

It was now 2 weeks since Tabby went missing. Despite Olivia's objections, Tony refused to give up hope. He agreed to end his quest after he looked into one final possibility.

There was no answer when he knocked on the door of his former home. Tony got back into his car, and drove next door to Grace's house, hoping she might have seen Tabby. Grace had always been fond of Tabby. She often watched Tabby when he and Ruth went out of town.

"Tony, can we please go home soon?" Olivia moaned. "I'm not feeling well."

"Yes honey, right after I talk with Grace," Tony said. "Thank you for being so patient with me."

The look Olivia shot at Tony indicated her patience had ended long ago.

Grace unlocked the door and opened it slightly. She looked over the couple and realized it was Tony. She figured that Olivia was the woman who triggered the divorce. Grace opened the door completely and saw that Olivia was in the late stages of pregnancy.

"Hello, Grace," Tony said awkwardly. "I'm sorry to bother you, but I'm hoping you might be able to help me. Tabby is missing, and I'm wondering if you might have seen him. He got away while Ruth was unpacking at her apartment in Newton Bay. Anyway, it's a long shot, but I'm looking into all possibilities."

"You don't know?" Grace said. "But then again, how could you."

"Know what?" Tony asked.

Grace sighed. She dreaded going over the story again.

"Ruth came looking for Tabby, just like you. She talked to the new owners, hoping that Tabby might have tried to return to your old house. I wish she had come here first."

Tony's stomach started to tighten.

Grace sat on the porch chair and proceeded to tell Tony the entire horrific story. Several times she stopped and wiped her eyes, as she tried to keep her composure.

"I wanted to go and rescue Tabby when he hid in the bushes. I knew he was hurt bad, but I was so scared of that man! When I finally got up the nerve to try, he came out again. I drew back and hid, hoping he would drive away so I could get to Tabby. But I never got the chance…"

A mounting rage was building up in Tony. Olivia was frightened as she felt his muscles tightening.

"Is there any chance Tabby might still be alive?" Tony asked.

Grace shook her head. "If Tabby were still alive, the boy and his friends would have found him," Grace said. "Tabby would not have been able to go very far."

Tony dropped his head. "What boys, and what friends?" he asked.

"That coward lied and told Ruth he knew nothing about the cat." Grace continued. "His wife came over here, just like you, to see if I had seen Tabby. She told me that their son and his friends were out searching for Tabby. I told his wife the truth, and what I thought about her husband. I should have kept my mouth shut!"

"Why?" Tony asked.

"She confronted him, and I heard them screaming and arguing. He was drunk again and lost it. I saw two girls who were the boy's friends leaving the house in a hurry, and I asked what happened. The girls saw the beast hit her so hard that her nose was bleeding!"

"Did you call the police?" Olivia asked.

"No, the man terrifies me! I figured his wife should call the police. Thankfully, she and the boy left while the brute was gone. I was sick. As I said, I should have kept my mouth shut, and that poor woman would not have been hurt."

The conversation was suddenly interrupted by the sound of a car entering the driveway next door.

"Is that him?" Tony asked Grace.

When she did not say anything, he knew the answer.

Olivia grabbed Tony as he hurried off the porch and walked toward Rick.

"Please, don't Tony!" Olivia pleaded. "Let's just leave. That man has already caused enough trouble. Don't get dragged into it. Not now, not when the baby is coming so soon!"

Blinded by fury, Tony yanked his arm free from Olivia's grasp.

"WAIT HERE!" Tony barked at Olivia.

But Olivia would not wait. She continued to try and pull Tony back. Tony continued to pull his arm away from her as he advanced toward the house.

Olivia had never seen Tony this angry, and it scared her.

"Please Tony!" Olivia begged. "It's not worth it. Not for a cat!"

Tony stopped.

"My mom's cat!" he snapped at Olivia. "A cat she loved dearly! The cat that helped her through cancer treatments!

The cat that comforted her during her roughest days! The cat she entrusted to me! Tabby was not just any cat!"

Tony continued walking as he watched Rick stagger into the house. As he approached the porch, he once more pulled his arm away from Olivia.

"Please, go stay with Grace!" Tony said through clenched teeth.

"No!" Olivia fired back. If you're not leaving, then I'm not leaving!"

The door suddenly opened, and Rick stepped out on the porch.

"Get the hell off my property!" he snarled.

CHAPTER 22

"Tony, please stop!" Olivia pleaded as he continued to approach Rick.

Rick stood at the doorway, while Olivia continued trying to pull Tony away.

"Listen to your lady and get out of here!" Rick snarled, as he turned and slammed the door.

Tony bounded up the steps and pounded on the door, breathing heavily as he waited for Rick to open it.

"Tony, I'm begging you, please stop, let it go!" Olivia groaned. She tugged at his arm, again meeting with complete resistance.

"Go back to Grace's house, NOW!" Tony ordered.

"What the hell do you want?" Rick snapped as the door flew open.

Tony's mind was now completely charged. He looked at the repulsive man, whose own rage was fueled by alcohol and the recent events in his life.

Tony moved Olivia behind him, and gave her a quick look, desperately hoping she would leave.

Olivia stood her ground.

"I'm looking for a wife-beating, cat-killing coward named Rick!" Tony said with clenched teeth. "He's good at hurting the weak and defenseless. Just stopped by to give him a taste of his own medicine!"

Despite his inebriation, Rick recognized Tony from the recent closing.

Rick delivered a sinister smile. "Well, look who came over to call the kettle black! If it ain't the wife-cheating adulterer and his pregnant whore!"

Both men stared at each other, as Olivia continued her struggle to pull Tony back off the porch. When Olivia started to cry, Tony reluctantly backed down the porch with her.

"That's right, get off my property, or I'll do to you what I did to that cat!" Rick yelled.

Tony yanked free from Olivia, as Rick started to stagger back inside the house. He grabbed Rick from behind and shoved him into a pillar on the porch.

"Well, I'm not your wife or a cat, so let's see what you got, you #@$%!" Tony screamed.

Rick lunged at Tony, catching him off guard, and sending both men hurling down the porch.

The punches started to fly; each man was so angry that they barely felt the blows delivered by their opponent. Olivia screamed through her tears, begging Tony to stop.

Blood began to flow from the combatants, as the intensity of the engagement increased. The fight was a sick therapeutic exercise, a channel used to release each man's pent-up anger. Pain and injury were inconsequential.

Olivia was terrified. Each time she drew near the fray, Tony screamed for her to leave.

Grace heard the screaming and commotion, followed by the thuds of fists hitting flesh. She feared for Olivia's safety and dialed 9-1-1.

Rick landed a solid shot to Tony's chest that sent him falling backward into Olivia. Without wasting a second, Rick charged into Tony, causing Olivia to fall, and both men landed on top of her. Olivia's head hit the ground hard, and the back of Tony's head hit her mouth. Tony quickly pushed Rick off to the side. Enraged by the assault on Olivia, he was fueled by a new burst of energy.

"Olivia, please! Get away from here!" Tony pleaded.

Olivia staggered to her feet, feeling dizzy, her mouth bleeding. She slowly made her way toward Grace's house, just as the squad car pulled up. Two police officers emerged and ordered the men to stop. When their order went unheeded, they attempted to separate them. Officer Riley locked Tony's arms behind him and pulled him back.

Rick took a wild swing at Tony and hit Officer Riley in the jaw. Riley let go of Tony, as he tried to work his slightly dislocated jaw back into alignment. Tony, now free, charged into Rick, ripping at his hair and delivering repeated shots to his face. Rick pushed a finger into Tony's left eye, forcing Tony to release his hair.

Both men were bent on destroying each other.

Riley and his partner had enough. They were now dealing with an assault along with resisting arrest. It was evident that these men were not going to surrender peacefully.

They pulled out their newly issued tasers and set them according to the training they received four days earlier. When a final warning was not heeded, the weapons were deployed. Both men dropped to the ground. They were quickly handcuffed and thrown into the squad car. They had their rights read on the way to the station.

Olivia collapsed a few yards from Grace's door, hidden from sight as the police vehicle sped away. There was blood trickling from her mouth, along with a new issue of blood moving down her leg.

The siren faded into the distance, as she lost her battle to remain conscious.

CHAPTER 23

Susan informed Lizzy that if Chance remained stable, he would be well enough to go home in about a week. When Lizzy informed Ben, he decided to arrange a "cat shower." Lizzy was not keen on the idea. She worried that Chance would need time to adjust to having people over. Ben cleared it with Susan, who said that Chance was used to the noise of the animal hospital, so a quiet party would be OK.

"Liz, don't worry," Ben said. "I'll take care of everything. I've already started a guest list, along with some suggested gifts. Just look it over and let me know if I missed anyone."

A mutual friend named Fred lived in the same building as Lizzy. He often watched Max when Ben and Lizzy were away. When Ben told him about his plans for the shower, Fred insisted that the food be served in his apartment. It would allow people to talk freely without disturbing Chance.

After the invitations were sent out, Sam sent Ben a text message, asking if he could bring a friend.

"Sure Sam, any friend of yours is a friend to Lizzy and me!" Ben replied.

"*Well, we'll see about that*!" Sam thought.

On the day of the shower, Ben set up refreshments, borrowed chairs, and bought some simple decorations. Lizzy organized her bedroom for Chance's arrival. Susan called and went over medications, and said that she would cover basic care for Chance once they had him settled in.

Friends gradually arrived carrying cards, gifts, and food, which were deposited in Fred's apartment.

In all the excitement, Ben forgot to tell Lizzy that Sam was bringing a guest.

Since most of the guests had arrived, Lizzy figured the knock at the door must be Sam. She walked briskly, preparing to chastise him if he brought a gift. She opened the door and froze.

There was Sam, standing in the hall with Marge.

"I hope we're not too late," Sam said, trying to break the tension. "We had to park down the street quite a way. Your friends have not heard of carpooling!"

Ben came up behind Lizzy, wondering why she did not invite the guests in. He saw Sam first, and then Marge.

"Come in, come in," Ben said nervously.

Sam took Marge by the hand, and the restaurant friends greeted him warmly. Sam introduced Marge to everyone, as she took a seat.

Ben closed the door and turned to rejoin the party, but was immediately stopped by Lizzy, who grabbed his arm.

"Kitchen!" she hissed.

Seeing that no one was watching, Lizzy shoved Ben.

"Hey, what was that for?" Ben said, somewhat miffed.

"Did you know about this?!?" Lizzy screeched.

"Yes and no," Ben said.

"WHAT does that mean?" Lizzy said while holding her forehead.

Ben explained that Sam had asked if he could bring a friend, but that he had not specified who it was.

"I'm sorry Liz, I never thought he would bring her. But please, don't get worked up and put a cloud on the party.

95

You have a lot of friends here who came to celebrate, including Sam. You need to compose yourself!"

Lizzy realized Ben was right. She took a deep breath, apologized, and thanked him for arranging the shower.

"I need a few minutes to pull myself together."

Ben nodded, and then shoved Lizzy.

"You need to reel in that physicality, at least until after the guests leave!" he said as he winked and left the room.

CHAPTER 24

Marge was nervously fixing her hair as she glanced occasionally at Lizzy. She wondered if agreeing to go with Sam was a huge mistake. But Sam had insisted; he said if she would not go, then he would not go. Ben saw how uncomfortable Marge was, despite Sam's best efforts to put her at ease.

Lizzy had greeted everyone, except for Sam and Marge. When Ben realized Lizzy was deliberately avoiding them, he went up behind her, and firmly held her arm.

"Kitchen!" he whispered.

Once in the kitchen, Ben took Lizzy by both hands and looked her in the eyes.

"Sam likes Marge. So, get it together! If you don't want to greet them, then I'll do it alone!"

She knew Ben was serious. And he was right. She had continued a feud with Marge that she should have ended shortly after it started. She was rude to Marge on the phone and during her visitations with Chance. The recent note she sent with Sam was mean and short-sighted. Her nasty, sarcastic side needed to be hauled in before things got uglier.

Still, she wished she had seen this coming, so she could have been better prepared.

Lizzy walked alongside Ben as they went to greet Sam and Marge.

"Thanks so much for coming," Lizzy said, shaking each of their hands. Ben said the same and then gave Marge and Sam a hug. Lizzy did not appreciate being upstaged, so she followed Ben's lead. The hug Lizzy gave Marge could best be described as "robotic."

Sam wanted to say something afterward, but he let it go.

After about an hour of socializing and refreshments, Lizzy's phone rang.

"I'm here," Susan said. "Would it be possible to send a few people down to help bring Chance up to the apartment? He has to be moved carefully. I'm double-parked outside the entrance."

Ben and two of the restaurant workers ran down to meet Susan. They carefully removed the kennel where Chance was sleeping and climbed the stairs to Lizzy's apartment. The guests quietly left Fred's apartment and watched as Chance was brought to the prearranged location in Lizzy's bedroom.

Lizzy lifted the blanket covering the kennel. Chance was unaware that he had been moved. Everyone quietly circled and looked in at the guest of honor. The cast on the broken leg forced Chance to sleep on his side. The torn ear was nearly healed, the shaved areas where the surgeries were performed were beginning to grow fur, and scars replaced the stitches used to close the gaping wounds. Most of the guests had not seen Chance until now. They were told that the cat survived a terrible ordeal. Upon seeing him, they realized the severity of what he had endured.

Susan entered the bedroom and asked the guests if she could have some time alone with Lizzy. The room emptied as the guests adjourned back to Fred's apartment.

Susan gently woke Chance and had Lizzy give him his oral medications. Chance moaned and was not happy with the training session, sensing that Lizzy was a newcomer. He hissed a little and cried, but Lizzy was able to complete the task.

"Great job!" Susan said. "He will grab you with his front paws if he feels a sudden sharp pain; don't be alarmed. He has no claws. It's a reflex thing; he seems to know that we are not trying to hurt him. Be careful that he doesn't bite. He will warm up to you once he gets to know you better. If he becomes too ornery, call me and we can make new arrangements until he is further along."

Susan then went over the detailed "care plan" item by item.

"I want him to start using his leg more," Susan said. "Place his food bowl and water a little further from his kennel every few days, as well as his litter box. I'm hoping the cast can come off in a few weeks. Unfortunately, he will always have a limp; it was a nasty break. But with some TLC he will adjust."

"Thanks so much!" Lizzy said to Susan. "How much do I owe you for the house call?"

"Well," said Susan, "since this is a cat shower, this is my gift."

Lizzy thanked Susan, then brought her to Fred's apartment so she could introduce her to everyone. After Lizzy described in detail all of the great work Susan performed to save Chance, the group applauded quietly.

"Thanks, everyone," Susan said. "I don't do it alone. I see you are getting to know Marge. Without her, I would have had to close my practice and find a new occupation long ago. She is the backbone of our hospital. She deserves the applause!"

A second quiet ovation was given to Marge. Ben was prepared to poke Lizzy if she did not participate, but it was unnecessary. Lizzy smiled and joined in.

As the gifts were opened, Lizzy realized how blessed she was to have so many generous, caring friends. Along with the usual cat products, there were creative gifts such as "coupons" to watch Chance once he was stable.

Sam's gift was a combination of several show and dinner tickets that were to be used to celebrate Chance's recovery. Lizzy looked at Sam, shaking her head, trying to chastise him with her eyes.

Sam just smiled. "You're welcome," he said tersely.

Marge nervously handed Lizzy a card. Inside Lizzy found a two hundred dollar "gift certificate" for the animal hospital.

"It's good for any services you need, follow-up visits, checkups, and medications," Marge explained.

Lizzy took Marge's hands and guided her to her feet. They then both embraced one another in a proper hug.

"I'm so sorry!" Lizzy whispered to Marge. "I don't deserve this from you. Thank you so much."

"No, I'm sorry!" Marge whispered back as if the rest of the group could not hear them. "I was so out of line. Please forgive me."

Sam gently interrupted their conversation.

"Look, let's say you're both forgiven." He quipped. "We need to move along here; there are more presents to open!"

Once the gifts were all opened, Lizzy thanked the guests for their generosity and assured them that everything would be put to good use.

"Everyone, Ben arranged this party," Lizzy said. "Trust me when I say that without him Chance would not have made it. I hope that Chance will one day know that Ben is his true hero." Lizzy said. "And he's my hero too."

Ben shrugged his shoulders. Then he held up his hand to stop the applause.

"Indeed, Lizzy speaks the truth; there is no argument that I am a hero, likely one of the greatest heroes you will ever meet," Ben said with a serious face. "Now, if I could just work on my humility...."

Lizzy and the others laughed, as Ben went and helped serve refreshments. Susan asked Lizzy if they could return to her apartment for a few more instructions. Once inside, Susan walked over to the mantle and picked up the picture of Max. Susan turned and looked at Lizzy with a sad smile.

"So, this is how Max looked before the attack," Susan said. "I remember him; I remember all those cases."

"You do?" Lizzy replied.

"You were so upset; so heartbroken." Susan continued. "You knew he was dying; a curse of the medical profession. We did not even have time to make him comfortable. I wanted so much for you to have a chance to say goodbye."

Lizzy held Susan's free arm, while Susan held the picture with the other. She never thought about how difficult it must be for veterinarians to see a beloved pet die. Many pets are lifetime clients, and the veterinarians grieve almost as much as the owners.

"It was horrible when my parents died," Lizzy replied. "But I did not have to endure seeing them suffer. The crash killed them instantly. While it was a crushing ordeal, I never blamed myself. But with Maxie, well, I cried for months. I blamed myself in a hundred different ways. I guess to some extent I still do."

"I went to the court proceedings," Susan said. "Judge Logan asked me to attend since I treated many of the pets after their attacks. I met with the boys before the proceedings started, and went through each case file with them. First, they got to see family photos of the pet, showing how much they were loved. Then, I showed them photos of when they arrived at the hospital. I held up X-rays and gave them details about the injuries they caused, and the extreme pain they inflicted. I told them about the permanent damage they did to the pets that survived. A counselor was with us; he monitored the boys and their reactions. It was a mixed bag. One of them, named Lance, actually seemed to enjoy hearing about the carnage."

Susan paused and then continued.

"The others, however, were impacted by what they were shown. One, named Pete, repeatedly broke down into tears."

"Was he sorry for what he did, or sorry that he got caught?" Lizzy asked.

"I couldn't tell," Susan said. "But a few weeks later, the counselor came to the hospital to update me on the boys. The one named Lance was cut loose after one of the fathers attacked him. The counselor and therapist argued that he needed extensive treatment, but there was nothing they could do to hold him. The judge still feels guilty, knowing his hearing incited the attack."

Susan paused and then continued.

"The counselor then told me about Pete. He felt that he was truly remorseful. He wanted to know if Pete could volunteer at the hospital."

"Wouldn't that be like having a child molester volunteer at a daycare center?" Lizzy seethed.

"Those were my initial thoughts. But the counselor explained that Pete was a follower, desperate for friends, who was recruited by Lance. After the first hunt, Pete wanted out. But Lance forced him to continue, and physically threatened him if he refused. When they were finally caught, Pete was relieved. At the same time, he knew he was a coward, and it cost some of those animals their lives."

"So, what did you tell the counselor?" Lizzy asked.

"I agreed to give it a try for a few weeks under strict supervision," Susan said. "He started by doing cleaning and stocking supplies. He took out the garbage, swept and mopped the floors, and pretty much did anything we asked him to do. Eventually, he was allowed to feed and visit some of the animals. He enjoyed talking to them. After three weeks, he asked if he could continue to volunteer."

"What did you tell him?" Lizzy asked.

"I have to admit, I was thrilled, since he was a very dependable worker. I told him we would love to have him continue. He still volunteers every week."

Lizzy felt the old anger rising. Susan seemed to be defending Pete. Susan sensed the tension.

"I'm sorry, that was insensitive of me," she said.

"No, you did nothing wrong. I need to let this go; I'm just not there yet." Lizzy said. "This Pete, did he ever take care of Chance?"

Susan slowly nodded her head yes.

"He was very kind to all of the animals under his care, but he took a special interest in Chance. He became his cheerleader, talking quietly to him, telling him to keep fighting. I could never prove it, but I think Chance responded to his encouragement. Pete was happy to hear that I was finally sending him back home."

"Does he know that Chance belongs to me?" Lizzy asked.

"I would never disclose that information," Susan said.

Lizzy looked at the picture of Max. He was eternally cute, harboring that inquisitive look, waiting for her to return home. But Max was gone, and Chance was here. In one of those twisted developments in life, a villain of Max became a champion of Chance.

"Can I meet with him?" Lizzy asked.

Susan sighed. "Let me think that one over."

"I promise I will be civil," Lizzy said. "Just ask Marge!" Susan chuckled.

"I'll let you know," Susan said. "For now, let's get back to the party."

The picture of Max was returned to the mantel. Chance was sleeping soundly as Susan and Lizzy quietly closed the bedroom door. Gradually, the guests left, each receiving a hug from Lizzy and Ben.

As Sam and Marge left, Lizzy thanked them again for their excessive generosity. She noticed new energy in her old friend, and it made her heart glad.

"I'm happy I got to meet Sam," Susan said as she was leaving. "He seems very special. I'm so glad that he and Marge are enjoying one another's company."

Lizzy helped Ben clean up. She then told Ben to rest while she went in to check on Chance and give him his meds.

Ben refused.

"Mind if I help?" he asked. "I'm going to need to learn eventually."

"Together, they prepared Chance for the night. Then, sitting together on the sofa, totally exhausted, they fell asleep in each other's arms.

CHAPTER 25

"Please, hurry, she's bleeding!" Grace stammered to the 9-1-1 operator.

"Alright miss, please remain calm; let her know help is on the way. Bring your phone with you so we can stay in contact." The operator instructed.

Grace explained that she only had a landline. She set the phone down and went out again to check on Olivia. Grace was out of breath as she hurried back into the house, her hands shaking as she picked up the phone.

"She moaned a bit. I can't bend down to help her; my knees and hip won't allow for it. I told her help was on its way, but I don't think she heard me…"

****

The silence in the squad car carrying Tony and Rick was broken when the radio came to life.

"Attention all available units, we have a medical emergency at 776 Elm Park Lane. A pregnant woman was assaulted and injured during a fight between two males; she is responsive but appears weak. An ambulance has been dispatched with an ETA of 7 minutes. Any available unit nearby please go to the residence to assist."

Tony panicked as he heard the address.

"Officers, you have to turn back!" he yelled.

His plea was met with silence. After giving Tony an angry look, the police officer on the passenger side picked up the radio.

"Station, this is unit 5. We have 2 suspects in our vehicle charged with resisting arrest, assaulting a police officer, and other charges. The suspects were involved in the injuries sustained by the pregnant woman at 776 Elm Park Lane. We are proceeding to the station to place them in custody. I then need to proceed to the hospital with Officer Riley, who has an injured jaw."

"Officer, you don't understand! That's my fiancé who is injured. That's our baby! My baby! I need to help her… please!"

Both of the officers continued to ignore Tony.

When Tony realized his pleas were falling on deaf ears, he looked over at Rick.

"If anything happens to Olivia or our baby, I'll kill you!" he sneered.

Rick looked at Tony and laughed.

"Look, friend, you brought the fight to me. Whatever happens, is your fault. Didn't you bring her with you? But if you want to demonize me to make yourself feel better, go right ahead! Just know there's a long line in front of you."

Tony wanted to lunge at Rick, but then he realized Rick was right. It was his fault. He placed Olivia in harm's way, and she paid the price. She was seriously injured, their baby was in jeopardy, and now he could do nothing about it.

When they arrived at the police station, everyone stared at the two men responsible for injuring one of their colleagues. Tony felt helpless as he complied with each instruction and then was escorted into one of the holding cells.

Rick was put in a separate cell and immediately demanded to see a lawyer.

"Do you have a lawyer?" asked one of the officers.

"No, I don't!" Rick snarled. "You have to provide me one, right? I want one right now, so I can get out of this hell hole!"

"Well, you can discuss all that at your arraignment tomorrow."

No one listened as Rick continued to rant about his rights. Desperate, he called the lawyer who handled the closing of the house. After getting the details of the arrest, the lawyer explained to Rick that his small firm did not handle criminal cases. He suggested a few higher caliber firms in the Twin Cities.

"You need lawyers who specialize in assaults, disorderly conduct, resisting arrest..."

Rick cut off the lawyer mid-sentence.

"What do you mean assault?" Rick yelled.

"You've been charged with assault," the lawyer said.

"They can't charge me for assault, the other jerk started the fight! He assaulted me!" Rick screamed.

The lawyer once more explained that Rick's case was beyond the expertise of his small firm. Rick unloaded a couple of curse words and hung up the phone.

He was promptly led back to his cell, with no hope of anyone coming to his aid.

CHAPTER 26

Lizzy was jittery. She was at the point in her clinicals where she would have more responsibilities with less oversight. Her assignment for the shift was the Emergency Room or ER for short. In the town of Parables, the ER was small compared to the big city hospitals. But it was a crucial oasis for the surrounding communities, where everything from heart attacks to farm accidents were regularly treated.

Ben arrived with his accounting books, ready to spend the evening looking after Chance.

"How do I look?" Lizzy asked apprehensively.

Ben rubbed his chin as he slowly circled Lizzy, looking her over like he was shopping for a car. He examined her uniform, lifting her arms and bending them at the elbow. He straightened her collar, all the while keeping a straight face.

Lizzy rolled her eyes and shook her head, wondering why she even bothered to ask.

"There, much better," Ben said. "Now, just one more thing."

He pulled out his comb and moved toward Lizzy. She grabbed his wrist before the comb made contact with her carefully styled hair.

"Don't even think about it!" Lizzy squealed.

"Liz, you look great! You rock the smock! But I think you need to work on just one thing."

"And what might that be?" Lizzy asked.

Ben smiled as he quickly pulled her close.

"Mouth to mouth resuscitation." He said as he kissed her.

The kiss abruptly ended when Lizzy burst out laughing.

"You're sick Ben!" She said, pushing him back.

"Yes, I am, and greatly in need of a nurse!"

"More like a therapist." Lizzy countered.

She thanked him for the laugh. It relieved some of the anxiety that was building up as she prepared to head out the door.

"Look, Liz, try to relax," Ben said. "Think about how those nurses and doctors would feel if they were starting to work at Creighton's. It would take time for them to match your dazzling speed at taking orders, delivering food, and executing proper coffee pouring techniques."

Ben gave her the "am I right?" look as he gazed into her eyes.

"Yes, yes, I know!" Lizzy replied. "But keep reminding me anyway!"

"It's all about experience Liz. That's why they have clinicals. And in a sense, you will be in clinicals your whole nursing career. At least if you want to keep up with the changes and try the different avenues nursing has to offer."

She pulled Ben in for a final hug.

"Where would I be without you?" Lizzy mused.

Ben widened his eyes and whistled.

"Phew Liz, I shudder to think! Let's not even venture into that nightmare!"

Lizzy went over the medications Chance needed. Ben told her not to worry, that Chance was in great hands.

"You may do more medical care than me tonight." Lizzy lamented. "Last time I worked in the ER it was pretty boring. Not anything like the drama on TV. If you believe those shows, a life-or-death case comes crashing through the door every few minutes, with everyone scrambling, alarms blaring, and people yelling. Truth is, that's more the exception than the rule in Parables."

"Hey," Ben said, "just remember the scout's motto: always be ready! It's a proven fact that the toilet paper always runs out when you need it the most."

"On that totally irrelevant statement, I'm out of here!" Lizzy said while shaking her head.

She could hear Chance whimpering as she walked toward the door. It broke her heart when Chance struggled to get to his food and litter box. The pain caused him to cry and moan, yet each day he continued to use the damaged leg.

Ben waved to Lizzy and went to check on him.

During the short drive to the hospital, Lizzy did her usual mental reviews. She was no longer in a classroom; this was the real deal. To date, she had not experienced anything beyond what she could handle. As with every nursing student before her, she felt slow compared to the more experienced nurses. Her mentors assured her she was doing great, and at this stage, it was more important to be thorough than fast.

She parked the car, looked into the rear-view mirror, touched up her lip gloss, and made some other final adjustments. Ben had ironed all of her scrubs while he watched football. It felt good to be wrinkle-free. She took a deep breath, locked the car, and entered the hospital.

As she made her way to the Emergency Room, Lizzy still hoped that there would be some action, so she could show her mentors what she was capable of handling.

As she reported for duty, a new thought entered her mind: *"Be careful what you wish for…"*

CHAPTER 27

The ambulance raced through the streets of Parables while the paramedics worked to stabilize Olivia.

"We have a pregnant woman, bleeding vaginally." The driver relayed into the radio. "She is having contractions and fades in and out of consciousness. She also incurred a blow to the mouth. We are pulling up to the bay now."

Lizzy listened to the radio call and joined the team who waited at the ambulance bay. The ER doctor gave everyone instructions as the ambulance backed in. The paramedics removed the gurney and wheeled it through the doors. Lizzy hooked up the blood pressure monitor and waited for the ER doctor to finish his initial exam. Olivia suddenly opened her eyes and began to panic. Instinctively, Lizzy took her hand and gently talked to her.

"Hi, you're at the Parables hospital, we're going to take good care of you. Is there anyone you would like us to call?"

Olivia looked at the group of medical personnel positioned around the gurney, and then looked back at Lizzy and shook her head "no."

"Alright," Lizzy said. "I'm here if you think of anyone. Please try to stay calm."

"*Stay calm.*" Olivia thought. *How?* Yet, there was something in Lizzy's voice, and the way she held her hand, that allowed her to relax a bit.

The doctor relayed more orders.

"Contact OB-GYN, we have an emergency delivery that we are transporting. I need labs as soon as possible; this patient has lost substantial blood and likely needs transfusions. Ok, let's move."

Lizzy walked alongside the gurney, continuing to hold Olivia's hand. As they neared the elevator, Lizzy tried to pull her hand away, but Olivia would not let go.

"I can't go with you," Lizzy explained. "I don't work in that department."

"Please!!" Olivia blurted, grasping Lizzy's hand even tighter. The tension in Olivia's body caused the bleeding to start again.

"Come along with us." The doctor ordered Lizzy. She joined them in the crowded elevator, and once more Olivia relaxed. As the doors opened to the OB-GYN department, the gurney was pulled toward the delivery room. Lizzy kept pace, praying that the young woman grasping her hand would survive.

"Don't leave me!" Olivia pleaded. The OB-GYN doctor looked at Lizzy and nodded his approval. Several nurses helped Lizzy gown up, and then she returned to Olivia, who was once again fighting to remain conscious.

The team determined that Olivia was in no condition for a normal delivery. A C-section would be risky, due to the amount of blood Olivia had lost. The lab work results presented another challenge. Olivia's blood type was O negative, and the hospital was in short supply.

The intercom relayed an urgent request for anyone having type O negative blood to please consider an emergency donation.

Two people were working with that blood type: the hospital receptionist, and Lizzy. Lizzy bent down and told Olivia that she needed to leave for a few minutes to make the donation.

"You're coming back, right?" Olivia asked.

"Yes, and if the tests go well, there is a good chance we will be blood sisters!" Lizzy said as she smiled.

"That would be great," Olivia said as she tried to return the smile.

Lizzy left the delivery room and immediately called Sam.

"Now what?" Sam answered, pretending to be grumpy.

"Hey Sammo, is your blood type still O negative?"

Sam paused and sighed.

"My goodness, Lizzy, you're scaring me! What kind of nurse would ask that?"

Lizzy chuckled. "Just checking, sometimes older men find that it changes when they go through menopause or drink too much coffee."

"You're pushing it, Lizzy!" Sam snarled.

"Sam, there is an emergency here at the hospital, and they desperately need our blood type. Would you be able to donate?" Lizzy asked.

"On my way," Sam said and hung up.

The hospital receptionist was finishing her donation when Lizzy arrived. Her blood was taken to be screened and crossed matched to make sure it was compatible with Olivia's blood. The receptionist and Lizzy smiled as they exchanged places. Lizzy answered the screening questions while her blood was being drawn. Once she was done, Lizzy told the technician that Sam was on his way.

"When you finish, be sure to wrap his arm with the hot pink bandage. Tell him it's the only color left."

Lizzy rushed back to the delivery room after her donation, where anxious faces were relieved to see her.

"She wants nothing done until you're with her." One of the nurses explained.

The emergency C-section could not wait. Both Olivia and the baby were in crisis. The remaining supplies of O negative blood were already being transfused, and the doctor hoped it would be enough to get Olivia through the surgery.

"I'm scared; I'm really scared!" Olivia whispered.

"I know," Lizzy said. "But you're safe now. These doctors are excellent. I'm here, so try to relax."

Olivia's abdomen was cleaned and draped, and general anesthesia was administered. Olivia's grip began to weaken as she slid into unconsciousness. The monitors for Olivia and the baby were beeping, confirming what the surgeon already knew. The procedure had to be completed quickly if mom and baby were to survive.

Lizzy watched as the staff worked in tandem to complete their tasks. The baby, a boy, was delivered through the incision, and the mouth and nose were cleared of fluids. He was then examined by a separate team to see if he sustained any injuries.

The placenta was removed and the incisions were closed with sutures. The last bag of O negative blood was hooked up, as the doctors worked to curb the bleeding.

"What is the status on the O negative blood?" the surgeon asked.

"We put a request to all nearby blood banks and hospitals," a nurse stated. "Everyone is short, but they will let us know what they can do. The donations made here are being analyzed and should be ready soon."

"We need some as soon as possible." the surgeon lamented.

"I have a close friend who is also O negative," Lizzy said. "He is on his way to donate."

The surgeon left the delivery room and waved for Lizzy to follow him.

"You're new here, aren't you?" he asked Lizzy.

"Yes, I'm doing my clinicals," Lizzy replied.

"Well, thank you for all you've done. The patient was traumatized, and that was making the situation much more serious. The fact you were able to get her to calm down may have saved her life. We're still not out of the woods, but the worst is behind us. I hope her family will arrive soon. Maybe a few of them have her blood type."

"I asked if there was anyone I could call, and she said no. The baby's father needs to know what happened, unless..." Lizzy paused. It dawned on her that Olivia may have been beaten or abused by the father.

"How long is your shift?" the surgeon asked.

"I have about 8 more hours," Lizzy said.

"One of the nurses suggested that you should stay with this patient, at least until we sort out everything and find out what happened." the surgeon said. "She needs to remain calm. You seem to have her confidence. If you're willing to do that, I'll get clearance from the ER and your instructor to let them know we need you."

Lizzy nodded yes.

"Thank you, keep up the good work." the surgeon said with a smile, as he walked away.

Lizzy walked past the nursery. Olivia's baby was still being examined. She quietly entered Olivia's room. Two nurses were hooking her up to monitors and taking her vitals. Lizzy asked if she could help.

"Sure!" they said.

They explained what needed to be done, allowing Lizzy to get some hands-on experience. The charts were updated; the IV and blood transfusion were checked. For the first time, Lizzy got a really good look at Olivia. The young woman looked terrible. Her body had extensive bruising from the trauma.

After pulling up a chair beside Olivia, Lizzy began to talk softly.

"Hey Olivia, my name is Lizzy. You had a baby boy. Rest up, and let me know if you need anything. I'll check every few minutes."

Olivia lightly squeezed Lizzy's hand, as if to say "thank you."

"What a day!" Lizzy thought. She looked out the window in time to see Sam exiting the hospital, his draw site wrapped in hot pink. She went out to the hall and called Ben.

"Hey Ben, I'm going to be here for quite a while tonight. They assigned me a patient who needs a lot of attention. Could you do me a big favor? Tell Sammo that you need to take him out to dinner since he donated blood. Go to Ricardo's; call ahead and let him know that Sam is not to pay under ANY circumstances. Compliment Sam's pink bandage, invite Marge, and tell him I love him. I'll pay you back for everything."

Ben sighed. "OK, will do. But I better call Ricardo ahead of time so he has my charge card before the meal. Otherwise, Sam is a beast when it comes to picking up the tab!"

"Perfect," Lizzy said. "Oh! One more thing if you don't mind?"

"I'm listening," Ben said.

"Tell him he may have saved a life."

CHAPTER 28

The caller ID showed it was Tony. Ruth prepared once more to tell him she had no news about Tabby.

"Tony, I told you...."

Tony cut her off.

"Ruth, please listen. I'm in big trouble. I'm in jail! I don't have time to give you all the details. Like you, I went back to check our old house to see if Tabby might have somehow made it back. He did; from Newton Bay!"

Ruth listened in silence.

"Well," Tony continued, "the guy that bought our house, Rick, is a drunken lunatic. He killed Tabby! Grace saw it all."

"That's terrible," Ruth murmured.

"Anyway, he drove up while I was talking to Grace ..."

Tony paused to gather his thoughts.

"Ruth, I lost it. It was Tabby! He never hurt anyone in his life. I remembered the promise *we* made to my mom, and when I pictured him dying a slow, painful death ..."

Ruth continued to listen in silence.

"I went to confront the jerk. Olivia tried to stop me. I told her to stay with Grace, but she refused. We started fighting; Olivia got in the way. I was so enraged..."

The knot in Ruth's stomach tightened to the point she had to sit down.

"We were tasered and arrested." Tony continued. "On the way to jail, I heard an emergency call on the radio – it was about Olivia. During the fight, that jerk drove me into her, and she fell underneath us. They said she was being rushed to the hospital, and that she was hurt bad and bleeding. I have no idea what happened to her or the baby. As far as the police are concerned, I'm responsible!"

"How does this all concern me?" Ruth stammered.

"Ruth," Tony said in an exasperated voice, "I need you to find out what happened. Please, could you go to the hospital? I'm charged with several felonies, and in all likelihood, I won't be able to make bail. One of the police officers was injured trying to break up the fight. Even if I could post bail, there is no way I would be allowed to see Olivia."

"You can't be serious!" Ruth said.

"Olivia's parents live far away and don't want anything to do with her. I don't have any family nearby, and my co-workers can't find out or I'll lose my job. It will get out soon enough. I'll be the gossip of Parables, most likely lose my job anyway…"

"Tony." Ruth interjected, "I can't. You know Olivia wants nothing to do with me."

"You have to go, Ruth." Tony cried. "I don't have anyone else. *She doesn't have anyone else!!*"

Tony continued to plead with Ruth. For some unknown reason, she reluctantly agreed.

"Ruth, if you're allowed to see her, let her know that I am in jail and that I never should have put her or the baby in harm's way. Please find out what happened to the baby.

I'll call back in a few days. Look, I know you hate me, and telling you now that I'm sorry must sound empty. Right now, I hate myself. Be assured I'm paying dearly for my sins."

Tony hung up the phone, while Ruth was left wondering when the nightmare would end. Her mom saw the look of despair on her face.

"Who was that?" she asked, knowing full well it was Tony.

"Tony. He's in jail."

Ruth proceeded to tell her mom the whole story, and then said she was driving back to Parables to see if she could check on Olivia and the baby.

"Ruth," her mom sighed, "do you think that is a good idea? After all you've been through, I think you need a break from all the stress. This is not your problem!"

"Mom, I need to go. A lot of this is my fault."

"Well then," Ruth's mom said, "I'm going with you."

CHAPTER 29

Weak and groggy as she woke up, Olivia asked for water. She groaned when Lizzy raised the bed. In addition to the pain, she was nauseous.

"How are you doing?" Lizzy asked.

"How the hell do you think I'm doing?" Olivia snapped, as she laid her head back and closed her eyes.

"*That was a dumb question.*" Lizzy thought.

After Olivia drank some water, she asked for the bed to be lowered. She let out a sigh and fell back asleep.

Lizzy continued her vigil: wiping Olivia's brow; charting her vitals; and doing everything expected of a good nurse.

Later that morning, the surgeon came into the room. After conferring with Lizzy, he gently woke Olivia so he could ask some questions and update her on how things were going.

"Hello Olivia, I'm Doctor Stern. I know you're very tired, but I wanted to let you know that you are going to be all right. You got here just in time. Your baby is also doing well. Both of you will make a full recovery."

"Let me ask you, Doctor, what is your definition of a full recovery?" Olivia asked, without opening her eyes.

"Well, you and your son will both recover, physically." Doctor Stern stammered.

Olivia started to weep, and her body began to shake. Lizzy took her hand and tried to get her to relax. Doctor Stern crept toward the door and mouthed an "I'm sorry!" to Lizzy.

"Olivia, I'm right here," Lizzy whispered. "I'm sorry we upset you."

"Have you seen the baby?" Olivia asked.

"Briefly, after he was born. I've been here since you got out of surgery." Lizzy said.

"Not an issue," Olivia said. "I'm glad he is healthy. He will be easier to adopt out if he is not injured."

Lizzy tried to not react to Olivia's remark. A lot was happening in her life, and at the moment, none of it was good. If Olivia needed someone to talk to later, she did not want to lose her trust.

Olivia wept quietly and then drifted back to sleep. A woman from admissions knocked lightly on the door and asked Lizzy to step out into the hall.

"Are you going to be here when she wakes up?" The woman asked.

Lizzy nodded.

"Could you ask her if she would like us to notify her family?"

Without thinking, Lizzy said she would.

The woman handed her a clipboard that held several forms with highlighted sections for contact information.

Eventually, Olivia woke from a restless sleep. Lizzy offered her some water and ice chips, which she accepted.

"So, are we officially blood sisters?" Olivia asked.

"Yes, I think so," Lizzy replied. "They don't list the donor on the bags so I can't guarantee it. But you needed a lot of blood, so it's likely they used mine."

"Thanks," Olivia said while sipping the water. "I feel like my body is going through a war. Does your blood have rapid healing ability?"

Lizzy smiled. "Yes, I believe it does. It also is known to increase intelligence."

Olivia smiled back. "Well, in that case, I could have used it a long time ago."

"Hey," Lizzy replied, "while you were asleep, someone from Admissions came by. They wanted to know if any family members should be contacted."

No." said Olivia, as she stared blankly at the window. "My parents have pretty much disowned me. Dad's a Pastor; doesn't look good to the flock when his daughter has an affair with a married man and gets pregnant."

Lizzy looked up from the clipboard. Olivia sensed Lizzy's surprise. There was an awkward silence, as Lizzy turned back to the clipboard, hoping she would find an appropriate follow-up question.

"What about your husband, I mean, the father?" Lizzy asked.

"I don't have a husband," Olivia said in a tense voice. "I thought you would have figured that out by now. The FAA-THER is the reason I am in here, and why I almost lost the baby! So, I don't think I should call him...would you agree?"

Lizzy's instincts told her to stop immediately; clearly, this was not going well.

"I'm sorry; I didn't mean to get you upset. If you think of someone to notify, let one of the nurses know."

"I thought you were my nurse," Olivia said, wondering if Lizzy was bailing.

"Well, not exactly. I'm doing my clinicals, but I'm almost a nurse. I was working in the ER when they brought you in." Olivia explained.

Olivia squinted as she read Lizzy's name tag. "Well, thank you Lizzy the almost nurse, for the blood and for being nice. I hope you don't think less of me because of my history. But I wouldn't blame you if you did."

"No! I'm sorry, of course not," Lizzy said. "I'm just glad that you and the baby will be OK. My shift is almost over. Can I drop by and see you tomorrow?"

"That would be nice…but don't feel obligated."

Lizzy squeezed Olivia's hand lightly. She took a pad of paper and pen and wrote down her phone number.

"Rest up as best you can. If you need someone to talk to, give me a call. I'm not supposed to do this, but I can still plead ignorance at this point. If you do call, use my code name, Rizzy."

Olivia rolled her eyes and smiled. "Thanks, will do."

Olivia watched as the only person who could even remotely qualify as a friend left the room. Scared and hurting, she had never felt more alone.

On her way out, Lizzy stopped by the nursery to see Olivia's baby. He was beautiful. She called Ben to let him know she was on her way home and asked how Chance was doing. After Ben said that Chance was resting comfortably, Lizzy asked if he was up for a late dinner.

"I have to take a rain check, Liz. I'm falling way behind on my class assignments. I need to get back to my place and pull an all-nighter, and then do a shift at the auto parts store."

In recent weeks Lizzy placed a lot of demands on Ben's time, especially since Chance arrived home from the hospital. Ben never complained.

"Ben, I'm sorry I had to pull you away again to watch Chance," Lizzy replied.

Ben yawned an "OK," told Lizzy he loved her, and then hung up.

Lizzy's mind was spinning as she walked to her car. She needed to talk to someone.

Sam turned on the light in his bedroom, his phone blaring. The tune "Shake your booty!" awoke him from a sound sleep.

"This better be good!" Sam growled as he hit the green button.

"Sam, we need to go to dinner again so we can replenish our blood supply." Lizzy blurted.

"I'll go if you meet my two demands!" Sam said.

"You got it," Lizzy replied.

Sam smiled.

"One, you pay, because you woke me from a sound sleep! Two, you change this dang song on my phone immediately!"

"Deal!" Lizzy quickly replied. "I'll meet you at David's in ten minutes."

"Twenty minutes!" Sam snapped. "Unless you want to sit with an angry man wearing dated PJ's!"

CHAPTER 30

Ruth and her mom entered the hospital and went straight to the information desk.

"We're here to see Olivia Sky," Ruth told the receptionist.

Olivia's name was typed into the computer. The room number came up, and visitor passes were printed.

"Are you related to the patient?" The receptionist asked.

"No, we're just friends." Ruth's mom quickly replied after Ruth flinched.

"Ok, no problem. There is a note here that visits are limited to 15 minutes. You should stop at the nursing station to make sure she is not sleeping or getting medical attention. If you think of someone, we could call...oh, never mind. We'd have to clear it with the patient first; HIPAA requirements."

Ruth and her mom started to leave when Ruth turned back.

"Could you tell me where the nursery is located?" Ruth asked.

"Down that hall, you will see the signs." The receptionist replied.

Ruth's mom caught up to her as she headed toward the nursery.

"Ruth, I don't think this is a good idea."

"Mom, it's OK. I need to know that the baby will be alright." Ruth said. "Besides, I'm certain that Olivia will not want to see me. She'll likely have me thrown out of the hospital. I told Tony I would try. When he calls back, I may be able to let him know the baby is doing."

"You don't owe him that!" Ruth's mom seethed. "He can send someone else to check on his bastard child!"

"Please mom," Ruth sighed, "I need to do this."

The nursery window was clear of visitors when Ruth and her mom arrived. Ruth scanned the room, and saw the incubator labeled "Sky." A nurse, checking on the babies, saw Ruth, and relayed some hand signals, asking if she would like to see the baby.

Ruth nodded.

The nurse gently picked up the baby boy and brought him to the window. He squirmed a little in her arms and then opened his eyes. Ruth watched as he scanned the new world he had recently entered, and then began to cry. His bottom lip quivered, as the nurse rocked him.

"That little guy is fortunate to be here," said Officer Riley, who walked up behind Ruth. He gave the nurse a "thumbs-up" after she mouthed to him that the baby was doing great. The nurse let Ruth take a final look, then took the baby away to be fed.

An emotional storm tore at Ruth from all directions. She was responsible for Tabby being killed and nearly had an innocent baby meet the same fate. Olivia had injuries that limited visits to fifteen minutes. Tony was in jail, facing a long sentence.

It felt like her revenge completed its deadly and destructive work, and it returned to drop its poisonous victory straight into her damaged heart.

"Say," Officer Riley interjected, "You're the woman I found on the side of the road, coming out of the woods, in the middle of a rainstorm? Ruth, I believe.... correct?"

"Yes," Ruth said. "Can I talk to you?"

"Sure, I'm not going anywhere." Officer Riley said. "I'm waiting to see how much damage was done to my jaw."

They went to the cafeteria, and Ruth asked her mom to wait at another table so she could talk to Riley alone.

"Where do I start?" Ruth muttered. "I guess the point where we first met is as good as any. I did not stop and wander into the woods to pee. But I think you already knew that."

Riley smiled. "Well, I had a hunch. But now that you came clean, I can finally close the case file."

Ruth's head hung low; she gave no reaction to his attempt at humor. Riley saw that something heavy was weighing on Ruth, so he sat back and let her talk.

Ruth told him everything. She went into the details of her divorce, the anger that her husband's infidelity ignited, and the incredible hurt she felt when she found out that Olivia was pregnant. She wanted revenge and found a way by getting custody of Tabby.

"That cat was so sweet…"

Ruth paused as she tried to compose herself.

"Hey, you don't need to tell me this if it's too hard," Riley said.

Ruth forced a jagged smile.

"Please, I need to tell you; for a lot of reasons," Ruth muttered. "And when I'm done, I have a favor to request."

"I left Tabby in the woods, knowing that his demise would decimate my ex-husband," Ruth said. "I wanted him to feel pain, to hurt as bad as I did. But the thunderstorm started, and I remembered Tabby, and how terrified he must be. He trusted me like I trusted my ex-husband. I turned around to search for him. You found my car when I was looking for him. I never found him."

Riley nodded.

"Somehow, Tabby made it back to our old home," Ruth said somberly. But he ended up dead anyway. My ex-husband found out that the new owner who bought our house killed him in a drunken rage."

Officer Riley interjected. "Excuse me, but is your ex-husband's name, Tony?"

Ruth looked up and nodded. It was then she realized that Riley must have been one of the arresting officers who had been injured during Tony's arrest.

"I'm sorry," Ruth said. "I'm responsible for you getting hurt too."

"I don't know about that," Riley said. "So, why are you here?"

Ruth told him about the call from Tony, and how she reluctantly agreed to try and see Olivia and the baby.

"Well, I'm afraid I can't allow that," Riley said. "I have to interview her to see if she wants to press charges against your ex-husband and the other gentleman he was fighting. I need to make sure she is protected from any further harm. Besides that, even if she agrees to meet with you, which I highly doubt, myself or another officer will have to be present."

"I understand," Ruth said. "I need to ask you something very important, Officer Riley."

Riley asked Ruth to wait a moment as he went to the cafeteria, and came back with two glasses of water. He took Tylenol to lessen the pain in his jaw. He folded his hands and waited to hear Ruth's request.

"I'll make this quick. I told you how all these terrible events happened because of me. I caused a chain reaction of damage that almost cost Olivia and her baby their lives."

"Yes, go on," Riley said.

"Well, I need to be held accountable. As far as possible, I need to remedy the damage I have caused. I'm wondering if the charges against Tony could be dropped, or reduced, or somehow brought against me. Tony needs to be given another chance. I caused him to act as he did. The baby needs a father, Olivia needs him, and I need to accept what has happened, and get out of their lives, completely."

Officer Riley sat quietly for a moment, contemplating how to respond to Ruth's request. He looked across the table at the tired, remorseful, defeated woman, who was paying dearly for her actions. She had requested a self-imposed penance, but it was a request over which he had no authority to grant.

"Ruth, first of all, let me tell you how sorry I am to hear about what you have been through. I see you learned the hard way what unresolved anger can accomplish; the consequences you're enduring are heavy."

Ruth forced down a drink of her water and waited for him to continue.

"What you are requesting, of course, is out of my hands. There was another officer involved in the arrest. He and I were unable to get control of the situation since your husband, or ex-husband and the other fellow refused to listen to us. We had no choice but to use our tasers. In this day and age, we avoid using force like the plague; but we had no choice."

Riley paused to gather his thoughts and then continued.

"As I mentioned, I have to see if Ms. Sky wants to press charges for the assault on both her and her baby. The fact that they both survived doesn't mitigate the seriousness of what could have happened."

Ruth let out a sigh as she realized Tony faced substantial jail time.

"I have to go," Riley said. "I'll speak with Ms. Sky tomorrow. After I talk to her, I'll let you know if she is open to seeing you."

Ruth left the cafeteria and rejoined her mom. They walked out of the hospital in silence.

As they neared the exit to the hospital, Ruth's mom put her arm around her daughter. They arrived home to find Ruth's father waiting. He had ordered pizza and was putting together a salad. Ruth and her mom decided not to tell her father about the attempted visit with Olivia.

"I hope I'm not out of line by saying this, but I'm going to miss that cat." Ruth's father confessed.

"He was one of a kind."

CHAPTER 31

Lizzy looked over the menu at David's 24-hour Restaurant. She ordered the walleye, along with a cup of decaf coffee. Sam ordered a slice of pie and a cup of half-caf, hoping he would be able to fall back to sleep. When the walleye arrived, Lizzy cut off a portion, placed it on her coffee cup saucer, and slid it over to Sam. When he tried to push it back, Lizzy blocked his progress.

"Do you want me to change your ring tone, or are you happy with the current selection?"

"That was not our agreement!" Sam complained.

He put a fork into the piece of walleye, ate a portion of it, and handed Lizzy his phone. She went through all the choices, and Sam went with the standard ring tone.

"Boring," Lizzy chided, "with so many choices, why not try something else?"

"You don't need choices for a phone to ring," Sam said sarcastically. "This world has way too many choices going on: toothpaste, peanut butter, ice cream flavors, coffee, laundry deter...."

Lizzy cut him off. "Message received, Mr. Stick in the mud."

Lizzy went back to eating her dinner.

"I have to admit; this is good fish. It's not as good as Creighton's, but it's a close second."

Sam nodded in agreement after finishing the portion Lizzy had given him.

"I just realized," said Sam, "this is the first time we have been together in a restaurant other than Creighton's. If I ask you for a refill on my coffee, don't get offended."

Lizzy smiled.

"So," asked Sam, "what is the purpose of this late-night dinner that disrupted my beauty and blood replenishing sleep?"

Lizzy gathered her thoughts while she dipped a french fry in some catsup. She wiped her mouth with the napkin, set it back down, and looked across the table at Sam.

"First of all, Sam, thank you so much for donating blood on such short notice. You may have helped to save someone's life."

"Yes, I know," Sam replied. "You already had that message delivered. I'm sensing that you have other matters you want to discuss. Am I correct?"

Lizzy nodded.

"Well, I don't mean to be blunt, but I'm pretty tired," Sam said. "So, if you want any expert advice, you need to spit it out."

"Sam, I have a lot to learn about nursing, especially when it comes to dealing with patients." Lizzy lamented.

Without using her name, Lizzy told Sam about Olivia. She told him how things were going well until the admissions person asked her to request contact information.

"Sam, I should have never agreed to do it." Lizzy wailed. "She has no one! I upset her when I asked about the father of the baby. That was the last thing she needed! She's so sore and weak; I forced her to share the whole bleak situation. She said she was going to put the baby up for adoption, and.... oh, I shouldn't be sharing this with you, Sam. You may hear more about her through the grapevine. You know how chatty the people of Parables can be."

Sam smiled as he looked at the nursing warrior across the booth.

"We never truly know anyone's story, Lizzy," Sam said. "This girl needed someone to be there for her, and you happened to be working when she arrived. I don't think that was a coincidence. The surgeon recognized that you were able to help her through a very difficult situation. You kept her from getting more upset than she did. Are you planning on seeing her again?"

"Yes, I told her I would stop by tomorrow. I also gave her my phone number. I'm not supposed to do that. I doubt she will call."

"Doesn't matter," Sam interjected, "you showed her you truly cared. It may not have been kosher with hospital protocol, but this poor girl needs more than just physical healing. You displayed the same mojo that makes you a great waitress."

"And what would that mojo be?" Lizzy asked.

"Compassion."

Lizzy finished her meal, and both she and Sam let out a yawn. It was late, and it had been a long day. The blood donation tired out Sam more than she realized. Lizzy stood and intercepted the bill before Sam could grab it. Rather than risk a wrestling match, she walked straight to the counter and paid it.

"I got the tip," Sam said as she returned.

"Too late, I already covered it." Lizzy countered.

Sam relented. "I'm too tired to fight."

Sam asked about Chance as they exited the restaurant and stopped near the door.

"He is eating a little better and getting better at climbing in and out of the litter box. He still cowers when I come to give him his medicines and check on his wounds. It's a slow process. There are still trust issues. When he does venture out of the room, I have to watch him with my peripheral vision, so he does not get spooked. Maybe I'm being over-optimistic, but I think he *wants* to get better. Not so long ago, I wondered if he just wanted to die, to have the pain end, and to be at peace."

Sam smiled. "Keep cutting him slack. The greater the trauma, the more time it takes to heal."

"How is Marge?" Lizzy asked.

"Well," he says, "she no longer has the urge to run and hide when you come to the animal hospital with Chance. So, you're building trust in that arena too!"

Lizzy playfully punched Sam's arm.

"Thanks again Sammo, go get some sleep, you look exhausted!"

"You do the same, and remember what I said."

CHAPTER 32

Judge Logan shook his head as he reviewed the case files in his hands. There was a time not so long ago when these types of cases were a rarity in Parables. Back then, crime was so low that it was said that the police issued jay walking warnings, just to have something to do.

The Judge mumbled to himself as he summarized the case in his mind:

"A veteran police officer nearing retirement is injured. Two men had to be tasered to break up the fight. A pregnant woman is seriously injured; the baby is delivered by emergency surgery. The father of the baby is one of the suspects arrested. The other suspect also argued with his wife a few days earlier and struck her in front of their son and his friends. An elderly woman, who was taped making the 9-1-1 call, was put through an experience that no one at her age should have to endure. A cat named Tabby was mentioned as the catalyst for the fight."

"Tabby, where have I heard that name before?" the Judge said out loud. "No, it can't be!"

But it was…the same cat involved in one of the bitterest divorce cases he ever presided over.

"Looks like the aftershocks are not over." Logan lamented.

He requested the divorce records be brought to his office, so he could refresh his memory. He had awarded custody of the cat to the wife, in hopes of putting an end to all the drama. The wife had been put through an ordeal that left her a bitter person. He had hoped the cat would bring her some peace.

"If I had awarded the cat to the ex-husband, could this whole mess have been prevented?" the judge wondered.

Once again, he was second-guessing himself, as he did on other occasions during his long career as a judge. But lately, he was doing it more often.

The judge found information relating to the case in his inbox. There was a picture of Rick's wife accompanied by a restraining order request. The swollen face, broken nose, and black eyes told the story.

After his arrest, Rick refused a breathalyzer test. The arrest report included a statement that both officers detected a heavy smell of alcohol. Two cocktail lounges filed complaints against Rick, one of which was supported by affidavits from twenty-eight patrons who witnessed Rick kick the manager, who was a former Marine.

"God bless America," Logan muttered. "Attack a Marine, and you do not only risk serious injury; patriotic people everywhere will throw you to the wolves."

Logan phoned Officer Riley, so he could get an update on his condition.

"Hello Judge," Riley said, "my jaw may have been slightly dislocated, but I'm expected to make a full recovery without surgery."

"I'm glad to hear that you're OK." Judge Logan replied. "And congratulations, you are officially the first officers to use tasers within the jurisdiction of Parables!"

"Well, I wish we did not have to go that route," Riley said.

The next day the Judge went over his notes so he could keep everything straight. The arraignments began as scheduled. Officers brought in Tony first. He was wearing the traditional orange jumpsuit. His face and arms had numerous cuts and bruises, confirming the severity of the fight. The doctor and dentist who examined him concluded the injuries were "non-life-threatening" and required no further treatment.

"Mr. Lambert, I did not expect to see you back in my courtroom so quickly!" Judge Logan snapped. "It appears that you are still having relationship issues."

Tony glanced at the judge, and then hung his head.

"I see that you do not have counsel with you. Do you plan to hire a lawyer, or would like the court to appoint you one?" Logan asked.

"I will hire my lawyer, your honor," Tony replied.

"Very well, Mr. Lambert," Logan said. "At this point, you are facing two assault charges: One for Officer Riley who was injured during your arrest; the other for Olivia Sky, who was severely injured during your battle with Mr. Carver. Further charges are pending. You can enter a plea for these charges, or you can wait until you talk to your lawyer."

"I plead not guilty to both charges," Tony replied.

"So noted, please enter the plea." Logan said to the court reporter. "Due to the injuries sustained by the victims, bail is set at $500,000."

Tony flinched when the amount was announced. He would need 10% of the bail amount to use for a bail bond, and he did not have $50,000. The judge mentioned "injuries sustained by the victims" as the reason for the high bail amount. Did that mean that both the police officer and Olivia were hurt badly? If so, he was looking at serious prison time.

As the officer began to take Tony back to his cell, he looked up at Judge Logan.

"Your honor, could you tell me how Olivia and the baby are doing?"

"No, Mr. Lambert, you are not privy to that information. You should have thought about that before you did the things that landed you in my courtroom! As of now sir, you are a defendant, and not entitled to know anything about the victims. Now, I suggest you stop asking questions or making requests until you talk to your lawyer."

Tony was led away by a guard, and Rick was brought into the courtroom. Rick had twisted his ankle and tweaked his left knee. He grimaced as he limped into the courtroom; his head pounding with a headache fueled by alcohol withdrawal. He desperately wanted a drink.

Once he was placed before Judge Logan, he cleared his throat.

"Your honor," Rick stammered, "if I may, I would..."

"No, you may not, is that clear Mr. Carver! You will speak when asked to speak. That is unless you want to add contempt of court to the charges you are already facing. Do you understand?"

Rick nodded, afraid to say "yes" after Judge Logan chastised him. He momentarily drifted into a haze and failed to answer the judge when he was asked about a lawyer.

"Mr. Carver, did you hear the question, do you plan to hire a lawyer?" Logan repeated, looking at Rick for a response.

"Yes, your honor, sir," Rick replied. "I will need a lawyer assigned by the court; the one I have does not handle this type of case."

"Very well, one will be appointed." Judge Logan replied. "I will go over the charges with you, and you can enter a plea for each charge, or wait until you talk to your lawyer. As of now, you are facing three assault charges. One is for Officer Riley who was injured during your arrest. One is for Miss Olivia Sky, the pregnant woman who was injured during your fight with Mr. Lambert. The third is for...."

Rick cut the judge off.

"I plead not guilty to both of those charges!" Rick yelled. "And I hope you're not going to charge me with assaulting that jerk that started the fight because..."

"MR. CARVER!" Judge Logan yelled from behind his bench, "if you interrupt me or talk out of turn one more time, you will be charged with contempt, and this hearing is over!"

Rick wanted to lash out at the judge, but somehow, he was able to reel in his rage.

Judge Logan waited a long time, his eyes glaring straight at Rick. He then continued.

"You also have a pending assault charge filed by a Mr. Gallagher, who owns the Nelson's Sports Lounge and Grill. NOW, Mr. Carver, if you so choose, you can enter a plea for each of the charges."

"Not guilty to all charges," Rick said quietly.

"There are also complaints filed by the manager of the Honeybee Lounge." Judge Logan said as he shuffled the paperwork that was piled up in front of him. "He will likely request a restraining order because he does not want you returning to his establishment."

Rick was having trouble keeping track of the charges. He was in hostile territory, and the judge and police officers were not happy that he injured one of their own. He needed help, and the only hope he had was to contact his wife, Shirley.

"Your honor, if I could just call my wife…"

"Not going to happen, Mr. Carver." The judge said as he cut Rick off mid-sentence. "She filed the most recent restraining order against you. I'm told assault charges are pending as we speak. So, you will not be calling your wife."

The severity of the situation was hitting home. There would be a trial, and Rick could face serious jail time. Now, in addition to his head pounding and his body aching, he felt scared.

Rick evaluated the mess he was in. He had no one. Even his drinking buddy Bill failed him. His family was tired of his escalating drinking problem and uncontrolled anger. If anything, they would welcome his predicament as an opportunity for him to clean up his act.

"Bail is set at $500,000. A lawyer will be in contact with you before the next hearing." Logan said as he organized the various documents.

Rick was led away by the guard. He barely made it back to his cell when he dropped to his knees and vomited into the toilet. All the station personnel looked on with disgust.

No one had mercy for the man who "showed no mercy."

Rick suffered in his cell, alone.

CHAPTER 33

The next day Lizzy knocked gently and then walked over to Olivia's bed. There was no need to ask "How are you?" Olivia looked forlorn and exhausted as she stared out the window.

"Has the doctor been in to talk with you?" Lizzy asked.

Olivia continued to look out the window.

"He stopped by this morning and told me everything was looking good and asked me if I had any questions. I told him just one. How did I ever let myself get into this mess?"

There was another knock on the door, as Officer Riley motioned for Lizzy to step outside the room.

"I'll be right back," Lizzy said.

Riley walked a few yards from Olivia's door and introduced himself to Lizzy.

"Hi, I'm Officer Riley. I'm one of the arresting officers for the incident involving Ms. Sky," he said as he extended his hand.

Lizzy shook his hand, trying to remember where she had seen him before.

"I'm wondering if she is up for some questions about what happened," Riley asked. "I have to complete a report, and I need to know if she would like to press charges. Do you know if she has a lawyer?"

"I don't know," Lizzy said. "You need to ask her."

Riley waited outside while Lizzy went back to ask Olivia if she was up for an interview.

"Not now, please," Olivia said. "I need a break from it. Ask if he could come back later."

Lizzy relayed the response to Riley, who was talking to Ruth and her mom near the nurse's station. Lizzy assumed they were friends of Olivia. After telling Riley that Olivia did not want to talk at this time, she returned to Olivia's room as Riley continued his conversation with Ruth.

"It looks like there are some other people who want to visit you." She told Olivia.

Olivia turned toward Lizzy with a confused look.

"Who?" she asked.

Lizzy said she did not know. She described the two women in detail, and Olivia immediately knew who the one woman was:

Ruth.

"What the hell is she doing here?" Olivia seethed.

Lizzy felt her stomach turn into a knot; another assumption blew up in her face. This woman was anything but a friend.

"I don't know," Lizzy replied. "I can ask them to leave if you like. The police officer or security will escort them out of the hospital."

Lizzy turned to leave when Olivia suddenly stopped her.

"Wait! Tell the one named Ruth that I want to see her."

Lizzy was caught off guard by the request. She froze, trying to figure out what to do.

"Look," Olivia said, "you can either ask her to come in here, or I will get up and go see her…"

Lizzy held up her hand and then hurried to the nursing station, where Riley and Ruth were still conversing.

"Are you Ruth?" Lizzy asked.

Ruth, surprised by the question, nodded.

"Ms. Sky asked if she could see you. Just so you know, she is in a fragile state, so if she gets upset you will have to leave." Lizzy said.

Ruth nodded again, still surprised that Olivia wanted to see her. She told her mom to wait at the nurse's station.

"I'm going to have to accompany you, so Ms. Sky knows she can ask you to leave at any time," Riley said.

Ruth knocked and entered the room with Riley, wishing she never agreed to Tony's request. Olivia turned and faced Ruth, as the two of them gazed at each other. Olivia looked terrible; there was no anger in her eyes, just despair.

"Why did you come?" she asked Ruth.

Lizzy waited by the door, and Riley stood beside her.

"Tony asked me to come, to see how you and the baby are doing. He called from jail, so he…"

Olivia held up a hand and gave a sarcastic laugh.

"Well, I'm glad you're here. You will be happy to know you won. I never want to see you or Tony again! Tell him not to worry, the baby will be adopted; he will have a decent set of parents. Tell him everything is wonderful! Isn't that right Lizzy?"

Lizzy stood at the door, not knowing what to say or not to say. While she struggled to come up with an answer, Ruth spoke up.

"Olivia, I know I don't deserve to ask, but if you let me talk for just a few minutes, I promise you that I will never bother you again."

Tears built up in Ruth's eyes as she waited for Olivia's response.

Olivia wondered what Ruth would say. She could not remember a time when Ruth had anything but angry and spiteful words for her.

"Ms. Sky," Riley interjected, "you're under no obligation to listen to her. She told me the history between you two, and if you like, I can escort her out of the hospital."

Olivia looked at Riley and smiled.

"I'll hear her out, officer. Lizzy can do her nursing thing while we talk. If I need you to escort her out, I'll have Lizzy come get you. In the meantime, would you be willing to complete an affidavit, starting with her statement that she will never bother me again?"

"Well," Riley said, "a restraining order might be the better option."

"I was joking," Olivia said to Riley. "Please leave for a while, so I can have a final conversation with this bitch."

Lizzy wanted to leave too, but Olivia insisted that she stay. Once Riley left, Olivia introduced Lizzy to Ruth.

"This is Lizzy, my blood sister, maybe the only person who cares about me. She did everything she could to save my life. In short Ruth, without her, this conversation would not be happening."

Ruth acknowledged the introduction with a nod.

"I know I don't have any say in what you do," Ruth began, "but I hope you will reconsider things after you hear what I tell you."

Olivia gave Ruth a gesture to get on with it.

"There's something you should know," Ruth said. "Tabby did not get lost. I left him in the woods, to get back at Tony. It was a terrible thing to do."

"Well, I guess I'm not surprised!" Olivia said angrily.

"As you know, the man Tony fought had beaten and killed Tabby," Ruth said. "In reality though, I killed him. I knew how much that cat meant to Tony. That's why I fought so hard to get custody; custody of an innocent cat who was already stressed by the loss of Tony's mom and all the fighting during the divorce. I wanted revenge. I *wanted* Tabby to suffer, so Tony would suffer."

Lizzy cringed at the idea of hurting a cat to get back at someone.

"So, you see," Ruth continued, "I was the cause of all this sorrow and pain. I wish they could press charges against me instead of Tony, but it can't be done."

"Why would you want that?" Olivia asked.

"Because I'm responsible. Releasing Tabby in the woods and hearing how he died did not help me feel better. Instead, it left me feeling empty and depressed. When I heard you and the baby also could have died, I realized the horrible impact of my decisions. I need to move on and let the past go. Enough damage has been done."

Olivia studied Ruth, searching for any hint of insincerity.

"What I'm saying is please don't make any decision about the baby yet. If you can, try to forgive Tony, and give him another chance. If I had gone my own way, none of this would have happened."

There was an awkward silence, and then Ruth got up to leave. She thanked Olivia for listening and reiterated her pledge to leave her and Tony alone.

Olivia was deep in thought until she drifted off into a deep sleep.

"Have I crossed the line again?" Lizzy pondered as she left the hospital.

She could request that she no longer be assigned to Olivia's care. However, she had gained Olivia's trust, and to bail now would be wrong. Olivia needed her. She had no one else.

Later that evening, Olivia woke and ate her dinner. The nurse came in to take the tray once she finished.

"Is there anything else I can do for you?" the nurse asked.

"Yes," Olivia replied. "I want to see my baby."

CHAPTER 34

Rick had never felt so sick. His body ached all over from the recent fights, while the pounding in his head was relentless. Nausea had him hugging the toilet. The dry heaves aggravated his sore ribs, and he grimaced and screamed during each uninvited session. A doctor was brought in to check on his condition. Dehydrated, Rick was `taken to a clinic for IV fluids.

His court-appointed lawyer was waiting for him when he returned. He took Rick to a nearby conference room and closed the door. The lawyer summarized the charges and sentencing guidelines and asked Rick if he understood what he was facing.

"What I need to know," Rick replied while rubbing his forehead, "is when I can get out of this joke of a jail."

The lawyer was familiar with cases like Rick's. The alcoholics, living messed up lives, whose only concern was how quickly they could return to their old ways. He needed to give Rick a reality check.

"Well, with good behavior, you could be out of prison in five to ten years. It might be more, depending on how much damage you did to the police officer, and if the woman who was pregnant presses charges. I see that during your arraignment you made a stunning impression on the judge. So that could also factor into the final determination."

Rick's nausea was replaced by shock. He looked up at the lawyer, hoping that he was joking around. But the lawyer had nothing but a solemn look on his face.

"By the way, sorry, my name is Frank." The lawyer said, extending his hand. "May I call you Rick?"

Rick did not want to shake hands. His demeanor turned to anger.

"Get me someone who knows what they're doing!" He yelled at Frank.

"Look, you want another lawyer?" Frank said. "Ask the judge at your next hearing. That should go over really well. Whether you realize it or not, Rick, you're at the mercy of the court. As bad as things are, you can make them a lot worse. But I don't want to waste your time or mine; I have other clients to see. If you want to hear my advice, tell me now, or I'm out of here."

Rick did not respond, so Frank packed up his files and got up to leave.

"Wait," Rick said, "Let's talk."

Frank sat back down and took out a notepad. He explained to Rick that the best chance he had to reduce his sentence was to agree to extensive long-term treatment. Even then, there were no guarantees; but courts are more sympathetic if a defendant agrees to take proactive measures to address the core problems behind the crimes.

"Think it over," Frank told Rick. "I'll be back in a few days to discuss specifics."

After looking at his watch and grimacing, Frank quickly packed his briefcase. As he got up to leave, Rick extended his hand for a handshake.

"Sorry for the outburst," Rick mumbled.

"Not a problem," Frank replied. "Just don't have another one in the courtroom."

CHAPTER 35

Lizzy let out a shout as she held the notification. She had passed her boards. She was officially a certified registered nurse. The hospital was holding a full-time position open for her, confident she would pass.

The long road was finally over.

She called Ben and relayed the good news. There was silence on the other end of the phone.

"Ben, did you hear what I said?" Lizzy said.

"Yes, I heard you. But make sure Lizzy. Sometimes they can get mixed up on those things and send people the wrong scores. I don't want to expend too much energy congratulating you until you're certain." Ben said playfully.

Lizzy shook her head.

"Yeah, I'll get right on that, Ben. In the meantime, get over here and give me proper congratulations! I'll have a punch waiting for both shoulders; so, decide which one you want first!"

"Hey babe, you know I'm proud of you! Always have been, and always will be. No need to resort to violence. I'm just trying to keep you humble. I'll be over in five minutes."

The packet included a letter stating that there would be a "Pinning Ceremony" for all of the graduates. There was a form to fill out, asking for the name and background information of the person chosen. After delivering the promised blows to Ben's arms, Lizzy asked Ben if he was OK with Sam doing the pinning.

"Liz, that's a great idea!" Ben said enthusiastically. "Let's be honest. Where would you be today without Sam? That man loves you like a father; he was as determined to see this day arrive as you were. Sam deserves that honor!"

Lizzy hugged Ben, relieved that he agreed.

"Besides, I don't think I could reach my arms high enough to pin you after those vicious blows you just administered," Ben said.

"Vicious?" Lizzy asked. "I was just getting warmed up. By the time I'm done, you'll be needing help tying your shoes!"

A playful bout of wrestling followed. It did not last too long. They did not want to wake Chance, who had a rough day. Lizzy was weaning him off some of his pain medications, and it disrupted his sleep.

They retired to the couch, both breathing heavily. Ben pulled Lizzy close, and finally got serious.

"Hey Liz, you know I am super proud of you!" Ben said. "You're going to be an incredible nurse. Just treat your patients like you treat your customers at Creighton's; not that you want repeat patients like repeat customers, but you know what I mean."

Lizzy smiled and knew exactly what he was trying to say. When they finally caught their breath, Ben looked over at Lizzy.

"Hey, there's something I need to talk to *you* about," Ben said.

Lizzy looked at Ben and saw a nervous look on his face. She suddenly felt a pang of panic. She knew him well enough to know when he was about to deliver some serious news.

She watched as Ben reached inside his pants pocket, and pulled something out, his hands shaking slightly. Before she figured out what was happening, Ben opened the box, dropped to one knee, and looked into her eyes.

"Elizabeth Candone, will you marry me?"

CHAPTER 36

Tony looked up as Officer Riley approached while manipulating his jaw, to alleviate the pain. Tony was hit with another wave of regret. If only he could do the day all over again. He assumed Riley was coming to let him know that Olivia was pressing charges.

"May I come in?" Riley asked.

Tony nodded, as another officer opened the cell door. Riley proceeded to sit on the lone chair in the cell, across from the bed where Tony was sitting. He sat quietly, studying Tony, trying to assess the man who was, as the saying went, "in a whole heap of trouble". Tony looked at Riley and sighed, waiting to hear the latest round of bad news.

"If you want a lawyer present, I can come back another time," Riley asked.

"Not necessary." Tony moaned.

"I've had some interesting talks with the women in your life," Riley said, his voice a bit slurred as he continued to move his jaw around. "You did an incredible job of hurting both of them badly. In my mind, you deserve the maximum sentence just for what you've done to them."

Tony closed his eyes, while slowly shaking his head.

"I talked to your ex-wife Ruth first, who was at the hospital at your request. She said you wanted her to talk to

153

your girlfriend Olivia, to find out how she and the baby were doing. That was a real class act on your part." Riley said sarcastically.

"I know, but I didn't have anyone else to turn to." Tony lamented.

"Yeah, and whose fault is that?" Riley asked.

Tony stared at the floor.

"Ruth talked to me before she talked to Olivia. She confessed that she had abandoned the cat in the woods because she wanted to hurt you as you hurt her. She regretted what she did, and went back to search for the cat, but couldn't find him. She also went back to your old house and spoke to the new owners, unaware that the drunk you fought had already killed him."

Tony listened but kept looking down at the floor.

"Long story short, she feels responsible for everything that happened. She has volunteered to take your place in jail, and take the rap for everything. What do you think? Should I lock her up, and let you go?"

"No," Tony said. "I drove her to do it. I hurt her. She trusted me. I betrayed her in the worst way possible. So, no, I don't want her to take my place. She deserves her revenge."

"Well," Riley replied, "I explained that was not an option. She could not take responsibility for your actions, even if what she did triggered the fight."

Riley paused and then continued.

"Anyway," Riley continued, "I needed to interview Olivia, to see if she wanted to press charges. Not that the list of charges against you isn't long enough, but she deserves her day in court too after what you and the other idiot did."

Tony held his head with his hands.

"Did the baby survive?" Tony asked meekly.

"What's it to you?" Riley demanded. "You weren't too concerned about the baby during the fight, even though Olivia asked you repeatedly to stop. So why do you want to know now?"

Tony looked up; Riley was waiting for an answer.

"I *don't* deserve to know," Tony said. "I was in this blind rage, and nothing Olivia said could stop me. That jerk had killed my mom's cat. But it wasn't just that; it was like all this pent-up anger rose, and nothing was going to stop me from confronting him. Now I wonder, what was I thinking? How could I not see that I was endangering Olivia and the baby? I lacked the common sense to just let it go and move on.'"

Riley shifted in his chair and continued the conversation.

"Olivia found out that Ruth wanted to see her, which was the last thing she needed to hear. She was about to ask that Ruth be thrown out of the hospital, but then she changed her mind. When Ruth told Olivia that you sent her, you can imagine what that did to her emotional state. Olivia decided it was over, and planned to put the baby up for adoption."

Tony flinched. The baby had survived. Would he ever get to see the baby? He faced serious jail time, and under the circumstances, Olivia would have a strong case for putting the baby up for adoption. How could he have been such a jerk?

Riley waited for his statement to sink in, and then he continued.

"Then, I guess you could say the unexpected happened. Ruth begged Olivia to reconsider. She said that she was responsible for the fight because she knew what the cat meant to you. Ruth told Olivia she was done causing so much pain. She promised Olivia that she would stay out of your lives, forever."

155

"Why did she say that?" Tony asked.

"I was wondering the same thing. I think when she saw your baby, she realized that, like the cat, he was nothing more than an innocent victim. She found out how incredibly destructive her desire for revenge had become. Instead of bringing her satisfaction, it was destroying her. So, she is moving on, and for that to happen she does not want to see you or Olivia again."

Tony took a deep breath and sighed. "What a mess."

Riley signaled to another officer, who walked toward the cell carrying a bag. The officer opened the cell and handed the bag to Riley.

"Here, put your clothes on," Riley told Tony. "I'm taking you on a supervised visit."

CHAPTER 37

Lizzy prepared to give Mr. Creighton the traditional 2-week notice, with an offer to stay longer if needed. She had spent a long time trying to come up with the right way to break the news. Yet, when she finally went into Mr. Creighton's office, it still felt incredibly awkward.

"Well, if you could stay on for a year or so, that would be great." Mr. Creighton said sadly. "I knew this day was coming up fast, Liz. Congratulations, I'm proud of you! Thanks for all your hard work. You'll always be welcome here, so please come and visit."

Lizzy smiled sadly as Mr. Creighton hugged her.

"Thanks for being the greatest boss in the history of restaurants," Lizzy said. "I'll be coming by. It will be strange placing an order instead of taking one. I hope you know this place did more than just help me pay the bills. I'll never forget it; I'll never forget you!"

"Well, that's all well and good." Mr. Creighton replied in mock anger. "But right now, I need you to get to work, customers are waiting!"

Lizzy snapped her heels and saluted Mr. Creighton, then left his office. As she looked over the restaurant, not much had changed over the years. She hoped it never would. It was a fixture in Parables, a carryover from better days. The restaurant still held its own against the large chains that were invading the town. The competition found it difficult to lure away Creighton's dedicated cooks and waitresses, along with their loyal customers.

That seemed destined to change. In all likelihood, Creighton's was on borrowed time. There was no one in Mr. Creighton's family willing to take over the restaurant once he decided to retire. Family restaurants demand long hours, hard work, and a seven-day commitment.

On the positive side, the property had grown in value, and it would provide adequate retirement funds for Mr. Creighton once that time arrived.

As the news filtered to the rest of the staff, Lizzy was congratulated repeatedly. Regular guests soon got the news and marked her last day on their calendars. Sam and Marge were sitting in Sam's regular spot, taking in all of the activity. Eventually, Lizzy was able to make her way over to them to take their order.

"What's all the fuss going on?" Sam chided. "We're starving to death!"

Sam and Marge gave her their order, while Lizzy poured them both a cup of coffee.

"Listen girly," Sam said, knowing how much Lizzy despised the term, "no offense, but if you can't improve your work performance here, you might want to consider another profession!"

Lizzy glared at Sam.

"Thanks, chump; I'll take that into consideration. Now move over before I pour the next cup of coffee in your lap. I have something to ask you after you apologize."

Sam shimmied over while feigning a clueless face as to why he needed to apologize. Lizzy slid into Sam as she sat down. Marge smiled at the playful bantering. Once it was clear that Sam was not going to apologize, Lizzy rolled her eyes, shook her head, and began to speak.

"Well first, there will be a graduation ceremony. I certainly want you both to come. I also have another request. There is a long-time tradition called the pinning ceremony, where each graduate is pinned by someone instrumental in their nursing school journey. So Sammo, I was wondering if you would do the honor."

Sam was caught off guard.

"What about Ben?" he asked.

"It was Ben's idea too," Lizzy replied.

"Well, I'll have to check my calendar," Sam said with a smirk.

Lizzy enjoyed the new feistiness that Sam was displaying since meeting Marge. But this was a bit inappropriate. She decided to reel it in, quickly.

"No need to check. I'll just ask Mr. Creighton. I'm sure he will be honored; besides, he has never called me girly.'"

Lizzy slipped out of the booth and walked briskly toward Mr. Creighton's office. Sam scurried out of the booth and raced to catch up with her.

"Whoa, Liz, I was just kidding! I would be honored to do the pinning!"

Lizzy stopped and faced Sam.

"And...?" she asked.

"And I am very sorry for using the term girly...."

"Apology accepted. I'll pencil you in for the ceremony. We all have to say a few words about the person we selected, so it's a good thing you cleaned up your act!"

Sam hugged her and kissed her on the forehead.

"Thanks, Liz," He whispered. "This means a lot."

"Thank you, Sam, it's the least I could do for everything you've done for me over the years!" Lizzy replied.

Lizzy went to place their order, as Sam returned to the booth. Marge looked over at him, and he let her know that he had accepted the offer.

"Great!" Marge said. "That is an incredible honor, Sam. I'm looking forward to it. And I learned something new about you today!"

"What was that?" Sam asked.

"You can move pretty fast when you need to, chump!"

CHAPTER 38

The baby was crying when he arrived in Olivia's room, announcing his desperate need for comfort.

"Alright, alright, little fella!" The nurse said. "Here's momma, so no need for tears."

The nurse gently lifted him, and carefully gave him to Olivia. He was beautiful. It hurt at first as Olivia tried to get into a comfortable position. Yet, as she held him and talked to him, her pain began to subside.

Olivia was fairly certain that Ruth was sincere, and that she would move on. She asked Riley to talk to Tony, to help her decide if he was worth another chance. She also called her parents, to let them know that they now had a grandson. She tried her best not to break down as she left a message on her father's voicemail, but she failed at the very end.

Lizzy came to the hospital to let everyone that know she had passed her boards. She was wearing her uniform since she had just been at Creighton's to take a group picture with the staff. There was a buzz of congratulations, and some playful tug of war as different department nurses claimed her as their own. One of the nurses tapped her on the shoulder and said that Olivia would like to see her.

Lizzy knocked on the door, which was closed for privacy since Olivia was finishing up her session of nursing her son. Olivia waved Lizzy over to the bed.

"Isn't he beautiful?" Olivia asked, her eyes glistening.

"He is beyond beautiful!" Lizzy squealed.

"Would you like to hold him?" Olivia asked.

Lizzy nodded. She gently lifted the baby, who expressed a bit of protest from being separated from his mom.

"Easy little guy, mama gave me permission," Lizzy said as she smiled at the baby. "Have you decided on a name, Olivia?"

"Well, I want to talk it over with his father," Olivia said.

Lizzy gave a confused look. But she knew better than to ask any questions. The attending nurse arrived to take the baby back to the nursery, obviously happy that mom and baby had finally met.

"Say, do you have a little time to talk?" Olivia asked.

"I have all afternoon," Lizzy said as she pulled up a chair. "I'm not working; I just wore my nursing uniform for a group picture at the restaurant where I work."

"I've decided to keep the baby. I'm also considering giving the father another chance." Olivia confided.

Lizzy nodded, hoping that Olivia did not ask what she thought about her revelations.

"I am concerned about Tony, I will admit," Olivia said with a serious tone. "I don't understand how he could get so enraged by a cat. I've never seen him that way."

"Well, I'm not going to defend him," Lizzy said. "But I had a similar situation happen to my cat, and I can somewhat relate to how he reacted."

Lizzy told Olivia about Max.

"I had to be restrained in the courtroom," Lizzy said. "I wanted to hurt them back. Max was my baby."

"Do you still feel that way?" Olivia asked.

"I've let it go; well almost. Max was not the only victim. The boys killed and injured other pets."

"Wow!" Olivia said.

"The judge punished them and had them meet all the victims, to see all the pain they had caused. He tried to administer some mercy, even though what they did broke a lot of hearts."

"Are you angry they were not punished more severely?" Olivia asked.

"Yes and no. The judge told us his rationale for what he did. I was still angry at the time. But I understood his objectives. Being a judge is a tough job. Anyway, nursing school and working at the restaurant helped me to get my mind off it."

Olivia enjoyed talking to Lizzy. She could not remember the last time she talked with another woman close to her age. It was so nice to share the excitement of her baby while not being judged.

"I overheard you passed your boards," Olivia said. "Congratulations, you're going to be a great nurse!"

"Thanks!" Lizzy said. "Hey, I better let you get some rest. That baby will be back soon for another feeding. I'll be back tomorrow night."

Lizzy straightened out the pillow and blankets for Olivia and adjusted the hospital bed to make her more comfortable. She turned to leave when there was a knock at the door. Officer Riley peeked in. Tony was standing next to him. They walked past Lizzy and stopped next to Olivia's bed.

"Is this a good time for a visit, Ms. Sky?"

CHAPTER 39

Rick felt another wave of anxiety building. The alcohol withdrawal was getting more brutal. He needed to escape, to be freed from the confines of his cell. He needed some fresh air; maybe a long walk, and, of course, a drink.

But there would be no drink. There would be no visitors, other than the lawyer that was appointed to represent him. No one was calling to see how he was doing. The station personnel did only the minimal amount of required contact with him: meals, showers, and cell clean-up.

For the king of self-denial, the reality was sinking in fast. He was a serious problem to his family, his community, and himself.

And he was alone.

It was almost midnight when Rick experienced his first-ever panic attack. It became so intense he was sure it was a heart attack. He called out to the guards, who ignored him. Soon he was yelling at the top of his lungs, gasping for air as he continued to clutch his chest. Finally, in desperation, he grabbed the bars and slammed his face against them.

The blow gashed his forehead, which sent blood spurting through the bars and onto the floor. He fell hard to the floor, yet barely felt the pain. He was trying to get back to his feet, when two guards, wearing protective gloves opened the cell and pinned him to the ground.

Rick was shaking as he stared into the light at the top of his cell. He was numb and scared. The guards continued to hold him down until the ambulance arrived. The paramedics administered first aid while they did a quick evaluation. Rick was then placed on a gurney, where his arms and legs were put into restraints.

"His heart is likely fine." said one paramedic. "He's probably going through withdrawals. Not uncommon for someone with his history. They'll do a full evaluation at the hospital."

The jail personnel looked on in silence as the paramedics finished their work and wheeled Rick to the ambulance. A police officer accompanied the ambulance to the hospital. Rick's condition and vitals were relayed over the radio. The ER doctor examined Rick and ordered that the gash be sutured. He was given medicine for the panic attack, which finally helped him to settle down and fall asleep.

When he awoke, Rick was once again nauseous. It took him several minutes to figure out where he was. He tried to move and realized that he was immobilized. He pulled as hard as he could on the restraints; the exertion triggered a shot of pain to his face and head. The nausea suddenly kicked in big time, and he vomited.

Rick's movements triggered an alarm. The policeman stationed outside the door walked in with the nurse and grimaced at the foul smell. Clean-up was impaired by Rick's yelling and thrashing, earning him additional time in the restraints.

A psychiatric evaluation was performed, and it concluded that the attack was prompted by Rick's alcohol withdrawal. He was given medications for nausea and anxiety, which allowed him to once more fall asleep.

Early in the morning, Rick was awakened by a calm voice.

"Mr. Carver," the nurse said, "you need to remain still. I'm going to ask some yes or no questions, and you can simply nod your head to answer. Try to move as little as possible, so you don't damage the sutures. Are you feeling nauseous?"

Rick stared at first and then nodded yes.

The nurse remained calm as she went through the questions and gave him his medications. When she was finished, Rick was locked into a blank stare. The nurse took his vitals, did her best to make him comfortable, and then, instinctively held his hand and gave it a gentle squeeze.

"Get some rest," the nurse said, "a doctor will be in later to check up on you."

Rick blinked and faked a smile as he closed his eyes, hoping he would never have to open them again…

After Lizzy finished up with Rick, a nurse pulled her over to the nursing station.

"That's the cat killer, the one who hurt Olivia and almost killed her baby!" The nurse informed her.

"I know," Lizzy replied.

CHAPTER 40

Marge was finishing up with a client when Lizzy arrived early for their lunch date. While she was waiting, Lizzy scanned the back area of the pet hospital and saw someone cleaning out a kennel.

He was older now; a scrappy young man, but Lizzy still recognized him. He looked up and saw Lizzy staring at him, and froze. There was no place to hide; Lizzy went behind the entrance area and walked straight toward him. Susan saw the encounter developing, and ran to get in between them before a scuffle occurred. Marge also joined the pursuit, once she figured out what was going on.

"Please Lizzy, let's just go to lunch," Marge said. "There's no need to start any trouble here."

"I'm not going to start any trouble, I promise." Lizzy said." I just want to talk to him."

Susan refused to move, shielding the young man behind her. Lizzy stopped, walked back a few strides, and put both hands in the air.

"Honest Susan, I come in peace. I don't have any ill intent." Lizzy said. "If he doesn't want to talk to me, I'll leave with Marge."

Susan looked back at the young man.

"I'll talk to her." He said sheepishly.

Susan decided to stay close, in case Lizzy was pulling a fast one.

"You're Pete, right?" Lizzy asked.

"Yes."

"I don't know if you remember me. My name is Lizzy."

"I remember you; I didn't remember your name, but I remember you from court," Pete said, as he shuffled his feet.

Lizzy was about to speak when Pete spoke first.

"Listen, before you yell at me, I want you to know that I'm sorry for what happened. I don't expect you to believe me. I wouldn't believe me if I were you. But what we did to your cat and all those animals, was horrible. I think about it all the time, especially since I have been helping here, at the hospital. I was a coward, allowing those pets to suffer so I wouldn't get beat up. What we did was evil, pure, and simple! Lance insisted it was fun; told me I needed to get a backbone. I don't know why I went with them. I'm glad we got caught."

Pete paused, unable to look up at Lizzy.

"Look, I'm finding some peace working here. I see how important these pets are to their owners. I can't undo what I did. I wish I could, but I can't. But it helps to be here."

Susan moved to the side, so Pete and Lizzy could fully see each other.

"I understand you took care of a cat named Chance," Lizzy said.

Pete nodded.

"He was in really bad shape. We thought he was going to die a few times. Susan taught me how to care for his wounds. One day, he held my finger with his front paws and licked it a few times. He seemed to like it when I sat and talked to him. I miss him now that he's gone."

"Well," Lizzy said, "I want to thank you."

Pete got a confused look on his face.

"For what?" he asked.

"Chance is my cat. He was almost dead when I brought him here. Susan said you were a big reason that he held on, despite all the serious injuries he was suffering. Without your help, he most likely wouldn't have made it. You were here for Chance so he wouldn't go through the ordeal alone."

Pete sighed.

"How is he doing now?" he asked.

"Better; he still has a long recovery, and it's not just his physical wounds," Lizzy said.

"What do you mean?" Pete asked.

"I mentioned he was nearly dead when I brought him here. He not only suffered physical abuse. He has emotional trauma that needs to heal. I think by talking to him as you did let him know that people are trying to help him."

Lizzy looked at Pete and a thought occurred; perhaps Max did not die in vain. Pete accepted full responsibility for his actions and took positive steps to show he was truly remorseful. He went from an abuser to an advocate. Lizzy walked up and hugged him. Susan and Marge moved next to her in case a surprise attack broke out.

"Pete, thank you so much for all you did. I want you to do one more thing."

What?" Pete asked.

Lizzy cupped Pete's face in both of her hands.

"Forgive yourself," Lizzy said. "Forgive yourself, and live your life. We all make mistakes."

As she walked toward the door with Marge, Lizzy turned and waved to Pete. Pete waved back awkwardly and returned to his work.

Just outside the door, Susan came up behind Lizzy and tugged her arm.

"Thank you!"

CHAPTER 41

The newborn baby boy had no way of knowing that the man holding him nearly cost him his life. Someday he might hear the story of his birth, how his mom nearly died, and how his dad had to be incarcerated. He might hear that he was so beautiful that all the young nurses wanted to hold him. But at the moment, all he knew was that he felt comfortable. He squirmed a bit and settled into his dad's arms.

Olivia watched Tony starting to enjoy the moment; it was time to start the interrogation.

"Officer Riley, would you like to hold the baby?" Olivia asked.

"I'd like that very much," Riley said.

"Well, what's new Tony? Or should I call you daddy?" Olivia asked, as her facial expression turned to hurt and anger.

Tony looked up at Olivia. Her face and arms had dark bruises. Her movements were hampered by pain. The piercing look she gave as her lips quivered left him speechless.

"Have I hit the point of no return with Olivia?" He wondered.

"Do you want to know what I have been through, Tony, since you and that lunatic were arrested? I started hemorrhaging after they took you away. If Grace had not seen me, I would have died there, along with our child. I've had major surgery, with no one to be there for me. I was scared out of my mind!! They had to scramble to find enough blood. Right now, when this should be one of the happiest times of my life, I'm lying here feeling like a truck ran over me. And then, to top it all off, you send Ruth to be your messenger! So, if you don't mind me asking, do you have any more surprises for me?"

The nurse walked in and said that the visit would need to end soon; Olivia was in no condition to get upset.

"You have five minutes; then we leave," Riley said to Tony.

Tony walked up to the bed. Olivia had tears rolling slowly down her face. She asked the nurse for some tissue.

"Olivia," Tony began, "I have no excuse for what happened. I acted recklessly. The fight was so senseless; it could never bring Tabby back. I take full responsibility for what happened."

Olivia turned to look at Tony. He looked terrible, but Olivia felt no remorse.

"I'm so sorry about sending Ruth, but I had no one else to turn to." Tony continued. "I didn't have my phone available to call anyone from work. The only number I remembered was Ruth's..."

"Is that supposed to make me feel better?" Olivia snapped.

"No," Tony stammered, "I messed up this whole situation from start to finish. And I don't deserve your forgiveness. But I want you to know that I do love you, as hard as that might be for you to believe. I don't know what will happen with the court proceedings. Whatever is decided, I'll get the help they recommend, whatever it may be. I'm just begging you not to give up the baby; not yet. But if you do decide that is what's best, I will understand. I still love you."

Olivia wiped her eyes and took a deep breath as if cleansing her mind before responding.

Riley looked down at the baby, who opened his eyes a bit. He had held a lot of babies; including his children and grandchildren. He wanted this child to grow up and flourish, and have a future. He listened intently to the conversation between his parents.

"There are a few things Ruth told me during her visit," Olivia said. "She told me that your cat never escaped while she was moving. She deliberately released him into the woods, to hurt you. She claimed that she had a change of heart, and tried to find the cat. But it was storming out, and she couldn't remember where she had released him. Am I on track, so far, Officer Riley?"

Riley looked up from the baby.

"Yes, more or less," he said. "I found her out looking for the cat in the woods. She claimed she had to pee, but I knew there was more going on than nature's call."

"Well," Olivia continued, "Ruth said that everything that happened was her fault. She wanted revenge; but when she realized the cat suffered a horrible death, it hit her hard."

Olivia shifted in the bed, trying to get more comfortable. Each movement caused her to grimace.

"Do you want me to get the nurse?" Riley offered.

"No, I'm OK," Olivia said. Then she continued.

"When you sent Ruth here, Officer Riley said she had seen our baby. Part two of the mission you gave her. Well, after she saw the baby, she assured me that she was done. Done with us; done with revenge; done with living in the past. She promised to move on. She also asked that you be given another chance."

Tony sat silently, taking in everything that Olivia was saying.

"Don't take this the wrong way, Olivia. She deserved her revenge, but only against me." Tony said. "I hurt her badly. The affair, the divorce, and the pregnancy were daggers in her heart. I don't wish her harm; I hope she can get her life together. I just want you to know that I don't hold her responsible for all that has happened."

"Nor do I," Olivia replied. "After she left, I felt sorry for her. It was brave of her to confess everything. I want to believe she is sincere."

"We need to go," Riley said to Tony. "Olivia needs her rest, and we've already stayed too long."

Tony took Olivia's hand, and caressed it gently, being careful to avoid the bruises.

"I'm so sorry Olivia, for everything," Tony whispered. "Please find it in your heart to give me one more chance."

Riley stood up and went to hand the baby to the nurse.

"Wait, "Olivia said, "I want to hold him."

Riley went over to Olivia and gently placed the baby in her arms.

"Do you think Ruth is telling the truth?" Olivia asked.

"Yes, I do." He replied.

"How long will Tony be in jail?" Olivia whispered. "I want to give him a chance; I think he is sorry. It's certainly not the best way for a baby to meet his father for the first time. Is there any way his sentence could be reduced?"

"I don't know," Riley said. "But if you are sure you want to give him another chance, I'll see what I can do."

"Thanks." Olivia sighed.

CHAPTER 42

Lizzy's last day was the busiest that she ever had. There was a continuous line of customers waiting to be seated. They were all there to say thank you, and goodbye.

The tips were outrageous. Mr. Creighton called her into his office when he heard Lizzy arguing with customers that they were giving her too much. Once inside the office, he told Lizzy to close the door.

"Don't insult my customers!" Mr. Creighton barked.

Lizzy was startled at the direct command and realized Mr. Creighton was not kidding. He took a deep breath and then continued.

"Lizzy, these people came here for you, to thank you for being their waitress and friend over the years. Don't deny them the opportunity. This is your last hurrah, and they want it to be special. So please stop the arguing, and just thank them."

What Mr. Creighton said went against Lizzy's principles. But Mr. Creighton was right. Tonight, a chapter in her life was closing, and the people who made it so wonderful wanted to show their appreciation one last time.

"Ok," Lizzy replied, "I'll grit my teeth and smile, even if I feel guilty!"

The night was a celebration. Customers gave up their seats so that others could have a turn to place their final order and say goodbye.

Lizzy was so busy that she never noticed Mr. Creighton slipping in and out, chatting with the customers. Eventually, she made it back to Sam's table, where he and Marge were finishing up their entrées. Included with their bill were two crisp one hundred dollar bills. Lizzy picked them up and began to look them over.

"Don't worry," Marge said, "it's not drug money."

Lizzy took both notes and held them up to the light.

"I'm not worried about that," Lizzy replied. "It's just that there have been a lot of counterfeit one-hundred-dollar bills going around, and you two seem very suspicious."

Sam set his coffee down and gave Lizzy a look of disdain.

"Keep it up Lizzy, and I'm going to put down another two hundred dollars, just to rattle your cage!"

"Save your money, you're going to need it," Lizzy said. "Marge, could you take this guy out and get him some nice dress clothes? I need him to look polished when he comes up on the stage for the pinning ceremony."

"Why I oughta…!" Sam blurted as his eyes widened.

Marge covered his mouth and ordered him to hush.

"I certainly will," Marge said. "He needs some new additions to his wardrobe, and this is the perfect opportunity. Do you think he will look good in navy blue?"

For the next ten minutes, Lizzy and Marge planned Sam's outfit. Sam tried to interject but each time he was shushed by both women. Finally, he gave up the fight.

"A human mannequin, that's all I am to the both of you!" he protested.

"Thanks, Marge!" Lizzy said as she got up to leave. It was then that Marge noticed the ring.

"Is that what I think it is?" Marge asked.

"Yes!" Lizzy squealed. "Ben asked me last week. He caught me completely by surprise! I'm glad somebody noticed." Lizzy said while glaring at Sam.

"Well...about time," Sam mumbled, and then broke into a smile. "Congratulations, I'm happy for the both of you!"

"Well Sam," Marge said, "that means we will need to do some extra shopping for clothes! There's a wedding in the future!"

Sam held his head in both hands as if facing a great dilemma. Lizzy laughed as she went back to work.

By 10:00 PM, Lizzy wondered if she should call a Brinks truck. She looked up as a flood of people came through the door, many of whom had been in earlier. Before she could figure out what was going on, the lights were dimmed, and Mr. Creighton came out of the kitchen carrying a plaque, while the staff wheeled in a large cake. Mr. Creighton waved to Lizzy to come closer, and then signaled for everyone to quiet down.

"Well, thank you everyone for coming back. What a great turnout! I, uh, am not too good at speeches. I spent two full weeks preparing this one."

Everyone laughed.

"Why are you laughing?" Mr. Creighton said. "I'm not kidding!"

He put his arm around Lizzy, as he tried to keep his composure.

"We call this a family restaurant. For many of you, that means a great place to come and enjoy a meal with your family. But it has a wider meaning. Many of us who work here consider each other family. When we have to put up with all the crap you deal out, it draws us closer together."

Another round of laughter ensued.

"It was six years ago, a young woman who was planning on going to nursing school came in and applied for an opening as a waitress. She admitted that she had no experience, but said she was a hard worker and eager to learn. She said if I just gave her a chance, I would not be sorry. I fell for her sales pitch; I fully expected her to quit within a few weeks. Now, finally, she is getting out of my hair!"

Lizzy gave Mr. Creighton a playful shot in the ribs with her elbow.

"What hair?" Lizzy responded.

Once the laughter died down, Mr. Creighton continued.

"Well, Lizzy has reached her goal. She has finished nursing school and passed her boards. She is now a nurse. So, I invited you here tonight, to ask you, will it be alright if she waitresses your table wearing a nurse uniform?"

A cheer rang throughout the restaurant.

"Seriously, though," Mr. Creighton said, "we are all here to say farewell to someone we love and appreciate. We know she will be a great nurse because through the years we have gotten to know her as an incredible waitress. She has been many things: a counselor; a friendly voice; a witty adversary when we try to engage her in playful bantering. In short, she has made our days brighter."

Mr. Creighton picked up the plaque.

"Lizzy, on behalf of the Creighton's Family Restaurant, thank you for being our waitress for these past six years. Thank you for somehow balancing the rigors of nursing school with the demands of our customers. The crowd here says it all; you will be missed. So please stop by whenever you can."

Mr. Creighton then handed Lizzy the plaque. It read, "The Best Nurses Were Once Waitresses!" Below was the picture taken in her nurse uniform with the entire Creighton's staff. After reading it and seeing the picture of all her friends, she teared up and smiled as she hugged Mr. Creighton.

"Thank you for everything!" she said to him. "I'll never forget this place; it will always hold a special place in my heart...and my stomach."

The crowd broke out in applause and then partook of the cake and coffee. As the night came to a close, the staff finished cleaning up, and Lizzy hung around to say a special goodbye to each of them.

Mr. Creighton waited at the door as Lizzy was leaving. She looked around, picturing the customers over the years, and all of the great memories. Mr. Creighton handed her an envelope that contained a gift card for the restaurant.

"This way you have to come back." He said as he gave Lizzy a sad smile.

Lizzy thanked him again, went to her car, and watched as Mr. Creighton turned off the lights, locked up, and exited through the back door for his short walk home. The parking lot that was full just an hour ago was now quiet. The light near the garbage container illuminated the area where she found Chance. This life chapter was now officially closed.

After sitting for a few minutes, she started the car and drove home.

She never noticed the car that followed behind her.

CHAPTER 43

Lance Dennison had Creighton's Family Restaurant on his radar for some time. The newer businesses brought with them their high-tech security. Mr. Creighton relied on an antique safe and bolt locks.

Tonight, he saw opportunity knocking. The dinner rush was outstanding, meaning there would be a lot of cash on hand. He sat quietly in a booth watching all the activity while making his plans.

But then, he noticed the reason for the unusually large crowd. It was a pretty waitress, collecting huge tips on her last night. She would be a much easier target and could include a bonus of a little fun.

He left his car lights off as he followed Lizzy to her apartment. When she was gathering up her things, he ran and hid in the bushes near the entrance.

In his haste, he had forgotten to grab his ski mask.

"*No matter*," he thought, "*it's dark, and this bimbo is clueless.*"

Lance had a sudden case of deja-vu. He had been here before. It was one of his first paintball hunts; a dumb cat that made it way too easy.

Lizzy was fumbling with her keys when Lance jumped out, grabbed her, and held the knife to her throat.

"Don't make a sound, hand over the cash!" He growled.
Something was familiar about the voice.

Lizzy looked at the face: the one she had memorized; the one that constantly smiled during the court proceedings; the one that terrorized the little girl.

"You're the scum bag who killed my cat!" Lizzy snarled.

"Shut your mouth!" Lance ordered.

Things suddenly got more complicated.

"*The 'bimbo' made a positive ID!*" Lance thought.

"If you don't hand over the money right now, you'll be joining your cat!"

"It's in the car," Lizzy said.

She dropped the keys as she went to hand them to Lance.

As he bent over to pick them up, she delivered a hard kick toward his groin but missed the intended target. She ran down the street, screaming as loud as she could. Suddenly, Lance grabbed her hard by the hair. Seeing it was futile to fight, Lizzy handed him the money.

He smiled, put the large wad of cash in his pocket, and pulled her to the ground.

"Thanks!" he said. "But now it's time to teach you some manners. Make any more sounds, and they will be your last."

He pinned her arms under his legs while holding the knife to her throat.

"*How could this be happening?*" Lizzy thought; it was unreal. A night of celebration had just ended. A morning of horror was starting to unfold. Lance was no longer a teenage punk. He was strong, powerful, and determined.

"*I told him that I knew who he was,*" Lizzy thought, "*how stupid!*"

This night was not going to end with a robbery and sexual assault. Lance would have to silence her. The unfairness of life hit her like a whirlwind.

Sam's heart would be shattered. Mr. Creighton would blame himself for the rest of his life. The hospital staff would have to replace the welcoming party with an autopsy and memorial service.

And then there was Ben.

Even if she somehow survived a rape, she had been saving herself for him, not this derelict. They had worked toward building a life together. She glanced at the ring he had given her; her arms hurt as Lance securely pinned them under his full weight.

Without warning, Lance lifted her by the hair and slapped her as hard as he could across the face. Lizzy tried to fight back the tears, but it hurt too much. Lance then held the knife in the air, thrusting it deep into the ground, barely missing her ear.

"Now, listen up. Each time you continue to fight, I'm going to hit you harder than you've ever been hit in your life. It makes no difference to me if I knock you out. You decide how all this goes down."

As Lance started tearing at her waitress uniform, Lizzy refused to give in without a fight. She screamed again and struggled to free herself. Lance formed a fist to deliver another blow.

"Have it your way." He said calmly, as he lifted her head by the throat.

Lizzy closed her eyes. She felt a charge go through her body that seemed to paralyze her. The pain was horrible. Was her neck broken?

She somehow opened her eyes, unable to move, and then looked at Lance. His arms were flailing, as he writhed in pain. Officer Riley pulled him off and pinned him to the ground while another officer handcuffed him. Other patrol cars quickly arrived, lights and sirens blaring.

Riley and his partner were the closest to respond to a 911 call reporting a woman screaming for help. They were going to charge Lance until he raised his arm, revealing the knife. They did not want to run the risk of Lizzy getting stabbed, so they snuck up and fired their tasers. Riley's partner hit Lizzy. It took several minutes for her to recover.

"Are you alright?" Riley asked as he helped Lizzy sit up.

"Yes, I think so," she said. "He has my money."

Riley retrieved the money and said he would need to enter it as evidence before he could return it to her.

"Once we process it, we'll get it right back to you," Riley said.

Lance quickly recovered from the taser and began to struggle with the officer trying to get him inside the police car. Riley said he would be right back, and went to help secure Lance.

Lizzy glanced down and saw the knife that Lance had buried into the ground. She pulled it out and quickly approached Lance, who was still struggling with the officers. She stopped in front of him and held the knife to his face.

"You forgot something!" Lizzy yelled, as she drew the knife back and thrust it toward Lance's groin.

Lance instinctively tried to cross his legs.

"Don't!" Riley and his partner yelled in unison.

Lizzy stopped two inches from Lance, whose eyes were now closed. She turned the knife away and handed it to Riley.

"I was just going to return it to him." Lizzy jested.

"I'm glad I did your cat in; so colorful, and so fun!" Lance snarled.

Riley yanked him away and read him his rights. Lance became more belligerent.

"YOU have the right to remain silent!" he yelled back in defiance.

He did the same for each of the lines in the Miranda warning, as the other police officers finally got him into a squad car.

"Son, you had better hope the judge locks you up for your protection," Riley said, "because when this town hears what happened...well, let's just say things could get uncomfortable for you."

Lizzy now remembered where she had first seen Riley. He arrested Lance and his gang shortly before they were about to kill a stolen puppy.

Ben came running from his car and pulled Lizzy into his arms. The bruise forming on Lizzy's face along with the torn uniform told the whole story.

"Are you OK!? I tried calling you and wondered why you didn't answer. When I heard the squad cars, my heart sank! I'm so sorry Liz, I should have ...."

"Ben, I'll be alright. It's my fault; I should have been more careful. I'm still acting like Parables is the same place we grew up in."

An ambulance arrived, and after an initial evaluation, Lizzy was taken to the hospital. Riley and his partner followed, and let Ben ride in the back. The emergency room staff waited anxiously for Lizzy's arrival. The ambulance report had them all stunned:

"Assault and attempted rape, victim's name is Lizzy Candone. She took a blow to the face and may have arm or shoulder injuries. She also sustained a full discharge from a taser."

As the ambulance pulled into the bay, the staff jumped into action. Lizzy was instructed to remain on the gurney until she was fully checked out. X-rays were ordered, and she was admitted overnight for observation.

"They say the third time's the charm," Lizzy said to Officer Riley as he took down her statements.

"What do you mean by that?" Riley asked.

"Well, the first time we met, you caught the boys that killed my cat, Max. The second time was at the hospital when you had to interview a patient of mine. And now, the third time, you saved my life!"

Riley wanted to tell her that she was being a little dramatic. But the fact was, her life was in peril. If the neighbor had not heard her scream, or if they arrived a few minutes later, Lance likely would have taken her life.

Playing that scenario in his mind, Riley could picture himself discharging his weapon, every round, even as Lance offered to surrender. It would have violated every protocol he agreed to follow, back when he took the oath to serve and protect.

"Get some rest," Riley told Lizzy. "I'm glad we arrived when we did."

"For both our sakes..." he thought silently.

Ben wanted to stay at the hospital, but Lizzy assured him that she was fine.

"You need to get back and check on Chance."

Ben was shaking as he kissed her goodnight and apologized again for not being there to protect her. Lizzy grabbed his hand to stop him.

"Don't do that, Ben, please! We can talk about this tomorrow. Take care of Chance, stay with him if you can. Text me later so I know he is OK."

Shortly after Ben left, a reporter came in from the local paper, to get some details on the attack. The reporter had done some quick research on Lance Dennison and found he was a suspect in other robberies and assaults. This had the makings of a major news story in Parables and the surrounding area. Officer Riley came back into the room and grimaced when he saw the reporter.

"Look, I told you," Riley said, "the case cannot be discussed until charges are brought. I gave you the details of the arrest. Can that be enough for now? Ms. Candone needs her rest."

The reporter reluctantly agreed and left her card with Lizzy.

Once everyone cleared out of her room, Lizzy said a prayer of thanks, and with the help of her medications, fell asleep.

CHAPTER 44

Olivia was improving each day. The recent events gave her hope. There were issues to face once she was discharged. Caring for the baby would be difficult since she would have restrictions. Income was another concern, with Tony being incarcerated. Even if his sentence was shortened, he likely would lose his job.

She was mulling over the challenges when Lizzy knocked at the door. Olivia smiled until she noticed that Lizzy was dressed as a patient. Upon closer inspection, she saw the bruised face and watched Lizzy moving her shoulders in circles, trying to relieve the pain.

"What happened to you?" Olivia asked in a concerned voice.

Lizzy gave a short version of the event.

"I'm so glad you're alright! That must have been terrifying!" Olivia lamented. "I know I'm just one among many, but I would have been crushed if anything happened to you. You're the closest person I have to a friend."

Lizzy smiled.

"What do you mean, closest thing, girl? We are friends! I'm lucky I've gotten to know you, and your beautiful baby. I'm hoping you will allow me to spend some time with him once you go home. My fiancé and I plan to have children down the road."

There was another knock at the door.

Olivia looked up to see her parents peering into the room.

"May we come in?" her father asked shyly.

Lizzy gently embraced Olivia in a hug as they said their goodbyes.

"Thanks for everything," Olivia said. "Let's keep in touch."

"You have my number!" Lizzy whispered.

Once Lizzy was gone, Olivia looked over at her parents, wondering about the intention of their visit. Her mom gave her an awkward hug and apologized when Olivia flinched. Her father followed with a gentler hug.

Olivia adjusted her hospital bed and waited.

"Where do I start?" her father said. "Liv, I'm so sorry for what I've done. When we heard what happened to you, to the baby, I felt sick. You're our daughter; I had no right to say the things I did, or threaten to disown you…."

"Threaten?" Olivia interjected.

For the next half hour, Olivia's father confessed his sins. He was a minister, a spiritual leader, someone that a person in need supposedly could depend on. Yet he let his concern for his reputation outweigh everything. He was, in his own words, nothing more than a hypocrite.

Olivia listened, noticing that her father was becoming more and more emotional, and Olivia could not help wondering if it was all an act.

"Did you put him up to this?" Olivia asked her mom.

"Honey, I'm as guilty as he is. I need your forgiveness too."

"Well, what about Tony?" Olivia asked. "He is the father of the baby, and he's going to be my husband. Can you both live with that?"

"Yes." Olivia's father said, without hesitation.

The conversation was interrupted by another knock at the door. A nurse brought in the baby and gently handed him to Olivia. She looked up at her parents, who were unsuccessfully fighting back tears. She covered herself as she fed her son, and when she was finished, she looked at her parents.

"Would you like to hold him?" Olivia asked softly.

CHAPTER 45

Judge Logan was in a different frame of mind since he got word of the assault and attempted rape. The incident with Lance several years earlier literally blew up in his face, and almost cost a woman her life. He blamed himself for the meeting he arranged with the victims that incited the attack on Lance by one of the fathers.

Lance was no longer a juvenile. He would be tried as an adult. Judge Logan would not handle the case. Lance was now a marked man in Parables. His case would likely be transferred to another jurisdiction, to allow for a fair trial. For now, he was in the custody of Parables.

At the moment Judge Logan was tied up with another case involving a possible second chance. He talked to the arresting officers at length. Officer Riley and his partner assured him that Rick, not Tony, delivered the blow that injured Riley's jaw. Both officers also said it was Rick who pushed Tony into Olivia.

Despite the revelation, Tony was not an innocent man. There were plenty of other charges, including disorderly conduct and resisting arrest.

The judge had another serious matter relating to the case. He was livid when he found out about Riley taking Tony on the supervised visit. It was illegal, it was unauthorized, and it could have gone wrong a hundred different ways. It did not matter that Olivia requested the visit, or that she was not pressing charges. Tony was still in custody, and Parables was under the State's microscope for their "outdated and old fashion" law enforcement techniques.

"Riley," Judge Logan said glumly, "If you ever do something like that again, be ready to lose your job, your pension, and face jail time. Don't test our friendship. These are different times, *difficult times,* and you as much as anybody should realize that."

The next day, Logan went with Riley to interview Olivia. He wanted to be certain that she and the baby would not be placed in harm's way by any decision of lenience.

On the ride back from the hospital, Logan and Riley relived the good memories, when Parables was a small resort town, with low crime and high quality of life. Parables was no longer that utopia, and it never would be again.

"You know Judge," Riley said, "I've been at this job for thirty-six years. Back when I was younger, my size and physique were enough to keep a situation under control. Now, my back hurts, my left knee is shot, and I feel like the last few years have taken a toll. I don't know everyone in town like I once did. Sometimes I feel like the Parables I once knew is now just a figment of my imagination. I need to face reality. I'm out of my league."

Judge Logan nodded.

"You and me both." The judge said. "How is your wife handling you working the night shift?"

"Not well at all," Riley responded. "Lately, when I work, she can't sleep. Telling her not to worry is useless. She demanded to know why my colleagues call me the "Taser Man". When I told her, it brought her anxiety up to a new level. She calls my cell phone almost every hour when I work, to be sure I'm safe."

"My wife is worried silly about me too." The judge replied. "I'm up late at night reviewing cases, and she keeps begging me to come to bed. The workload keeps getting heavier and more complicated. Even when I go to bed, I usually don't sleep well."

It was on that ride back from the hospital that both men came to the same conclusion; their wives and families had been through enough. It was time to retire, enjoy the fruits of their labors, and hand over the reins to the next generation.

But first, there were loose ends to tie up.

The judge interviewed Tony several times, with Tony's lawyer present. Tony's employer agreed to let him keep his job, which was a key factor.

I'll be honest with you, Mr. Lambert," the Judge said, "I'm struggling with your case. I've had similar cases like yours unravel; I'm much more cautious now. So, the only way you will be released is if you agree to strict probation."

Tony listened as the judge outlined the parameters. He was to attend counseling to deal with his anger issues. He was to check in every two weeks with his parole officer. There would be surprise visitations to the house, to ensure that Olivia and the baby were safe. If, after two years, there were no incidents or problems, the charges would be dropped, and Tony's record would be cleared.

When Tony and his lawyer agreed to all of the provisions, Judge Logan authorized the probation. After completing the paperwork, Tony left the courtroom and headed to the hospital to see Olivia and his son. They still had not given the baby a name, but under the circumstances, that was likely a good thing.

Tony arrived at the hospital and walked into the room. He saw Olivia's father holding the baby. Olivia's mom looked up and gave Tony a nervous smile.

Tony kissed Olivia, as Olivia's father handed the baby to his wife.

"Congratulations." Olivia's father said as he extended his hand toward Tony.

"Thanks."

The difficult steps of reconciliation were underway.

CHAPTER 46

Grace watched as the last of her things were put into the moving van. She looked at the empty house that held over forty years of memories. So much had changed.

Her daughters were excited that she had finally agreed to move closer to them. They worried constantly about her safety, and the recent events sealed the deal. Grace faced the reality that things easily could have gone the other way. If Olivia had died, she would have never been able to live with herself.

She took a slow walk around the property and entered the yard where a beautiful garden once flourished. She had to give it up; her arthritis was too painful. The fence needed fixing or replacement. While her front porch kept things looking respectable, there were patterns of neglect everywhere.

She looked down the driveway at the nearby homes. At one time, she knew everyone in those homes. Now, there was no one she knew very well. All the surrounding neighborhoods had young couples who were busy with work and engaged in the lives of their children.

"*Too busy for a lonely old fool like me.*" Grace reasoned.

She went inside the house, entering each room, recounting to her daughters what it was like when they were little, living at home, and enjoying the numerous friends that

194

the "baby boom" era had provided. They both assured Grace that they had the best childhood anyone could ever ask for: A wonderful home, in a wonderful town, back when Parables was still a "Best Kept Secret."

As she walked through the living room, she pictured Tabby with her cats, running and playing, enjoying their time together.

"He was such a good cat."

Her cats were waiting in the car, watching to make sure that she would join them. She walked out and closed the door behind her, stepping away from the past, and walking into an uncertain future. She glanced down and saw blotches of dried blood where Olivia had almost died, a memorial of terror that would remain until the rains eventually washed it away.

"OK, time to go," Grace said, trying to force a smile to hide her breaking heart.

CHAPTER 47

The city council of Parables felt it was their civic duty to protect the jail from any upgrades. Visitors and citizens alike thought the archaic jail was a nifty "blast from the past". It brought back memories of "The Andy Griffith Show," where the town drunk could let himself in and out of the jail cell simply by reaching through the bars and grabbing the keys.

The police department felt it was adequate for their needs... at least for now.

As one of the last original buildings in town, it was given historical status. The plans were that one day it would be converted into a museum or a library to support the ever-growing population of writers and artists.

State entities were continuously urging Parables to enter the modern age of law enforcement. Violent crime was steadily increasing. Yet the fight to hold on to what was left of the original Parables guaranteed that each attempt to upgrade would be met with passionate pushback.

Recently, due to a higher number of arrests, prisoners had to be doubled up in the eight cells within the jail. Lance was placed in the same cell as Rick, so they could be monitored by the staff. Rick was feeling better and decided to strike up a conversation.

"So, partner, what brings you into the friendly confines?"

Lance proceeded to deliver a litany of curse words at Rick.

"Unless you want me to do some additional work on your ugly face," Lance said, "mind your own business, and shut up!"

Lance sauntered to the other side of the cell. Rick was about to confront the young punk when he noticed two police officers approaching the cell, along with a man dressed in a suit.

It was Rick's lawyer.

Lance was told to turn around and place his hands through the square opening in the cell door, so he could be handcuffed. Once he was secured, the door was opened, and he was brought out by the two police officers.

"Hi, Frank!" Rick said to the lawyer in a pleasant tone.

Frank gave Rick a quick nod, and then returned his attention to Lance. They went into a private room and closed the door. The conversation immediately turned tense. Lance was not cooperating and had to be subdued a few times. He was upset by what Frank was telling him.

"Look!" Frank yelled, "get this through your head. You are charged with armed robbery, attempted rape, and aggravated assault with a weapon on a nurse! A very popular nurse, I might add! This town wants to see you fried! And that's just the beginning. You're now been connected to some other crimes as well. Now sit still and listen!"

"Did you say rape!" Lance yelled. "I never got to finish with her!"

Frank sat back, while Lance began a long, continuous rant. He wanted a counter-charge of brutality filed against the police for using the tasers. He demanded to be moved to another jurisdiction. He wanted to be freed on bail, or on his own recognizance. He rattled off every benefit he had ever heard used on television, while Frank just shook his head, wondering if he had even a remote possibility of talking sense to Lance.

Rick, in the meantime, could hear the whole conversation. Lance was scum, a low-life rapist. Frank said it clearly; the whole town wanted him gone.

In his twisted morality, Rick saw an opportunity to become a hero.

Lance was eventually brought back to the cell, and once the cell was locked, he was instructed to turn around and put his hands through the opening so the handcuffs could be removed. Suddenly, Rick pulled Lance into the locked cell, turned him around, and began to slam his head against the bars. Still handcuffed and caught off guard, Lance could do nothing to stop the vicious blows.

One of the officers grabbed the keyring and went to reopen the cell door. Rick pushed a staggering Lance to the floor. He then picked up the chair and drove the legs through the bars. He hit the officer square in the chest just as he put the key into the lock. Rick reached around the bars, grabbed the keys, and threw them to the back of the cell.

"Help! Get the backup keys!" The officer yelled.

Several other officers ran into the holding area and saw Rick violently slamming Lance's head into the concrete floor. They pulled their tasers and tried to get into range. The first taser was fired and hit Lance, whom Rick used as a shield. The shocks sent Lance into convulsions; Rick released him in time so that he would not be shocked. Another officer prepared to fire his taser.

"Don't, he's too far away, we can risk hitting the other prisoner again!"

There was a frantic search for the other cell keys. Rick knew he had to act fast. Lance was unconscious, his face barely recognizable. From a sitting position, Rick wrapped his arm around Lance's neck and squeezed. Filled now with self-righteous zeal, he applied pressure with everything he had, and let out a scream as he crushed Lance's windpipe.

The police officers realized a murder was unfolding before their eyes. The senior officer pulled his gun and positioned himself to get a clear shot at Rick. Lance was completely limp as Rick continued to finish him off.

"Let him go, or I'll shoot!" the senior officer yelled.

Rick ignored him, and instead took Lance's head and twisted it violently, breaking his neck.

After a second order was ignored, the shot was fired.

CHAPTER 48

Ruth wandered through the shelter, unsure if she should adopt a dog, and if so, which one? Her mom thought it was too soon, and that maybe she should just volunteer at the shelter.

As she walked through the noisy kennels, Ruth noticed a quiet Jack Russell named "Rascal," who lay on his bed, trembling. Each time she went by his kennel, he followed her with his eyes; Ruth could see he was scared and confused.

"What's the story with him?" she asked the volunteer.

"A sad story." she said, "His family had to move out of the country, and they were not allowed to take him. They tried desperately to find him a good home. Their little girl was sobbing uncontrollably when they dropped him off. Rascal was crying too, trying to get back to her. The family thought it was best to leave quickly in hopes of minimizing the trauma. He has the sweetest disposition, but obviously, his heart is broken."

"Can I meet him?" Ruth asked.

"Sure! If you like you can take him for a walk around the fenced area. Be sure to talk to him, he likes to hear his name."

Several large dogs barked menacingly, causing Rascal to cower as Ruth walked him to the yard. He kept close to Ruth during the walk, looking up at her every few steps to see if his pace was OK. After walking for twenty minutes, Ruth sat on a bench and picked him up.

"Rascal, you should know upfront that I'm a mess. I'm not a good person. I'm the worst. But you may not have much time left, so you need to give me a chance. I hope somehow you understand!"

Rascal looked up at Ruth, and gently licked her tears. He was a good dog who recognized when someone needed his help.

"I'll take him," Ruth said to the volunteer when they returned.

The papers were signed, fees paid, and the items the family left behind were given to Ruth. There were medical records and notes on his shots, along with some of his favorite food. At the bottom of the bag was a picture of the family, along with a note:

"We hope that Rascal is in good hands. He is the greatest dog, and it will take us a long time to adjust to life without him. Please let him know that we will always love him and that we are very, very sorry!"

It was a short adjustment period for Rascal. He welcomed the long walks that Ruth needed, and the visits to the dog park allowed him to burn off excess energy. Ruth continued to tell Rascal what an evil person she was, and how the therapist was trying to help her let go of the past, but she was having trouble with that... all the while Rascal seemed to listen intently, giving an occasional lick to let her know he was present and concerned.

Eventually, Rascal became a celebrity at the Newton Bay dog park. Everyone enjoyed his playfulness and antics. Ruth found herself laughing whenever Rascal enticed the entire pack of dogs to chase him. One by one they ran out of gas. He would then trot up to Ruth for water, and lie down to let her know he was spent and ready to leave. People would come up to Ruth, and thank Rascal for providing some great entertainment. Friendships started to develop, and social invitations followed; Newton Bay was starting to feel like home for both Ruth and Rascal.

Once they arrived home and retired to the sofa, Rascal would jump up and lick Ruth's face, as if to say, "What a great day!" Then, he would curl up next to her in a ball of contentment, and snore softly once he fell asleep.

There were times when Rascal would peer out the window, searching for the little girl who was once under his charge. Ruth saw the sadness when he kept these vigils. At those times, she would retrieve the picture, and place it in front of him.

"Hey buddy," Ruth would tell him, "I hope you know they love you, and that the little girl right there, she *really* loves you! I promise that if they ever return, I will let you go back to them if that's what you want."

Her therapist smiled when Ruth told her this tale of self-sacrifice.

"Ruth," the therapist said, "it's highly unlikely the family will ever return. And even if they did, they would soon realize that Rascal has fallen in love with you too; they would have no choice but to let him continue to be part of your life. He's all yours now, so love him without reservation and stop with the improbable scenarios."

At night, Rascal would snuggle in the bed next to Ruth, and she would continuously pet him. When she eventually stopped, Rascal would look over to see if she was asleep.

Only then would he let out a sigh, close his eyes, and dream about the little girl.

CHAPTER 49

Lizzy started her Pinning Ceremony speech by talking about her parents, and how their death in a car accident solidified her decision to become a nurse. She choked up when she said how much she wished they could see this day, and sharing the moment with her. Some people at the ceremony heard about the recent attack and were surprised at her willingness to still participate in the program.

Lizzy then talked about how she met Sam, sitting in a booth, waiting for a cup of coffee. He asked her why she looked so tired, and she told him how she was going to nursing school.

"The road to a nursing career looked impossible at that point," Lizzy said. "Sam became a regular customer. He was genuinely excited when I shared my progress with him. He gave me generous tips and gifts on my birthday and Christmas, so I could continue to work toward my goal. As the years went by, he supported me, encouraged me, and provided timely wisdom. He was a parent, a cheerleader, and a reliable and trustworthy friend. I realized that along the way, my quest to become a nurse became his quest. He started as a friend, and now he is family; my family."

Lizzy paused and looked out at Sam.

"The world needs more people like Sam. Without him, I would not be standing here today."

Sam stood as the applause started, looking sharp in his new suit. Marge handed him a tissue so he could dab his eyes. As Sam drew near to Lizzy, they both smiled through tears, and whispered to each other to "stop it!"

Marge had practiced with Sam, and he placed the pin on Lizzy like an old pro. Then the two hugged, celebrating the end of the long journey.

After the ceremony, Lizzy was leaving with Sam and Marge, when she saw Ben standing at the back of the hall, looking strange. Was he upset after all that he did not get to do the honor of pinning her?

"What's up?" Lizzy asked.

"Lance Dennison is on life support," Ben said. "He's not going to make it. His mom is on her way to see him."

Ben told them what he knew about the incident. Lance was attacked by another prisoner who beat and strangled him. The other prisoner was shot during the altercation. The facts were still coming out, but the news was spreading quickly throughout Parables.

"Liz, don't get upset with me, but to be honest, I'm glad it happened," Ben confessed.

Lizzy knew that Ben was struggling. He blamed himself for not being there; for not taking her home; for not protecting her. "What if" scenarios were bombarding his mind. Lizzy knew that Lance Dennison's death would not end it.

"There's more," Ben said. "They have a team of surgeons heading to the hospital since his mom consented to honor Lance's commitment."

"What are you talking about Ben?" Lizzy asked. "What commitment?"

"Lance designated on his driver's license that he wished to be an organ donor."

Lizzy shook her head. It was nothing short of bizarre. She did not want Lance to ruin the moment. But she needed Ben to get past it, at least for one night.

"Ben, I think we need to go to counseling," Lizzy said.

Ben froze with a look of panic in his eyes.

"Marriage counseling?" he stammered, thinking Lizzy was having second thoughts.

"No! Of course not! We need counseling to deal with what happened. It won't go away on itself; we need to get professional help. Both of us need to go, together. Are you willing to go?" Lizzy asked in a hopeful voice.

"Yeah, of course, Liz. You're right, we need to get this fixed. Because I never want you to think that I'm a coward, or that I would be afraid to put my life on the line for you, because…"

For the first time since the incident, Ben broke down.

Lizzy signaled to Marge and Sam to leave and meet up later.

"Ben Odim, don't you EVER talk that way! I know the man I love, and he's no coward! He's the bravest, kindest, most reliable man I know!"

Lizzy pulled Ben in, kissed his forehead, and assured him that he was and always would be the only man for her. When he finally got his composure, Lizzy asked if he still wanted to meet Sam and Marge.

"We *have* to celebrate!" Ben said. "You, Sam, and I have waited too long for this day not to celebrate."

As they exited the hall, Lizzy showed Ben the deposit slip for the tips she earned.

"Wow, Liz!" Ben said. "That's incredible! Maybe you're being too hasty replacing waitressing with a nursing career."

"I'll think about it." Lizzy jested.

CHAPTER 50

Shirley entered the funeral parlor with Matt and her parents. The news of Rick's death was surreal. She had not been given much of an explanation. The bullet that took Rick's life was fired because he was killing another prisoner. The other prisoner was rushed to the hospital and was not expected to make it.

Somehow a lawyer got her number and said Shirley had a solid case for the use of excessive force. One prisoner heard Lance threaten Rick before the altercation. Several other lawyers also tried to call, so she turned off her phone.

The story was on the local and state news. The main focus was on the old jail; cute on the outside, dysfunctional on the inside. State and Federal officials arrived to go over every detail of the incident. Their reports would have conclusions and recommendations that would seal the fate of the antiquated jail.

Matt was enduring another round of guilt and turmoil. Rick was gone, and once again he felt partly responsible. He told his mom over and over again that he did not hate his dad.

Shirley was fighting with her own emotions, trying to prepare herself for the difficult time ahead. The funeral director led them to Rick's viewing room.

"Mrs. Carver, we really would recommend a closed coffin viewing. Our staff did the best they could, but there was extensive damage." The director said.

The truth was that Rick's damage was beyond the capabilities of the small-town funeral home. They had to call a funeral home in Minneapolis for assistance, who did the best they could on short notice.

A wedding photo was placed on the casket. It was an incredible dichotomy, the picture of a young couple celebrating the start of a new life together, and the casket ending any hopes for the future.

Shirley's first memory of Rick was of a young, loving, good-looking man who was enchanted with her. Her last memory of Rick would be the sick, angry man who struck her without any remorse. In between those memories was a slow trail of decay and destruction.

Matt approached the casket and drew next to his mom. His dad was gone, and with him went the last possibility of a relationship he still secretly cherished. He wanted to stay by his mom's side, to begin his new role as the man of the house. But he couldn't because he wasn't a man yet.

He was a ten-year-old boy who just lost his dad, and it hit him hard.

Shirley watched as Matt drew away and slowly walked out of the parlor. Anger welled up once more as she remembered all the broken promises, and all the attempts Matt made to function with a damaged dad. Matt's grandfather started to follow Matt when suddenly Shirley threw the wedding picture against the wall, shattering the glass.

"Damn you! Damn you, you bastard! Damn you," Shirley yelled.

Shirley stopped suddenly, and collapsed on the coffin, sobbing, as her mom rushed to comfort her.

****

The official start of the viewing was 1:00 pm. The only sound in the parlor was the ticking of the clock. None of Rick's drinking pals came to pay their respects. The two cocktail lounges where Rick was evicted held a macabre toast to his demise. And though the notice did not state that the viewing was for family only, everyone assumed it was.

Shirley's parents were shuffling back and forth, constantly asking Shirley and Matt if they needed anything, and bringing them food and drinks, which went untouched.

The viewing was scheduled to end at 5:00 pm. At 4:30 pm, the funeral director offered some prayers, and once again expressed his condolences. Matt watched the clock and realizing that time was running out, walked up and stood before the coffin. Tears hit the polished surface as he began to say goodbye to his dad.

"Dad, I'm going to miss you. I hope you know I forgive you, and I'm sorry I tore up your picture. Don't worry, I'll always consider you my dad."

He stretched his arms across the coffin, in an attempt to somehow give his dad a final hug.

At 4:48 pm, Chrissy, Matt's friend, arrived with her parents. They quietly entered the funeral home and made their way to the parlor. Chrissy's father scanned the room, and seeing Matt, grabbed hold of Chrissy's hand.

"It's almost 5:00 pm, let's give them some privacy."

Chrissy attempted to pull her hand out of her father's grip, but she could not free herself as he tightened it and pulled her toward the exit.

"I need to talk to Matt!" She yelled.

"Keep your voice down!" her father hissed as he yanked Chrissy's arm.

"My God, Vince, you're going to hurt her!" Chrissy's mother cried as she grabbed his arm.

Chrissy pulled away and ran into the parlor. She went straight to Matt and wrapped him in a hug. The two friends held each other tight.

Chrissy's father went to retrieve her, but her mother refused to let him get by.

"Vince, I swear, if you don't leave her alone, we're through! Now get in the car!"

Vince looked up to see everyone but Chrissy and Matt looking at him. He left the parlor and went to the car.

Chrissy's mother went up to Shirley, hugged her, and told her how sorry she was for her loss.

"Would it be alright if I leave Chrissy with you until later tonight?" she asked.

Shirley nodded and thanked her for coming.

Chrissy continued to hug Matt, waiting for an opportunity to tell him what was on her heart.

"Matt, I'm so, so sorry. I miss you."

"I miss you too," Matt told Chrissy. "I'm so glad you came. I feel so lonely Chrissy. I can't believe my dad is gone; I hope you understand. I'm sorry you had to see what he did to my mom. He was sick, so sick Chrissy…"

"Matt, I'm sorry that I could not come earlier," Chrissy said.

At 5:00 pm sharp, the funeral director said a few additional prayers. He expressed his condolences again to Shirley and the family and offered them the opportunity to say their final goodbyes. Chrissy waited while Matt and his mom paid their final respects.

Matt's grandparents gathered up the flowers and cards that had been sent by relatives and friends. The coffin was removed so that preparations could be made for the next funeral.

"Mrs. Carver," the funeral director said, "I will contact you when the cremation is over and the remains are ready for pick up."

"Thank you," Shirley responded as they exited the funeral home.

After a quiet dinner, it was time to take Chrissy home. The time had passed too quickly, and Matt wished she could stay longer. Both friends got out of the car when they arrived at Chrissy's home.

"Say hello to everyone," Matt told Chrissy. "Hey, it means a lot to me that you came today. Thanks so much ..."

Chrissy held Matt's hand as he walked her to the door.

"I'll call whenever I can Matt," she said.

Shirley listened to their pledges and promises as they walked slowly to the door. Her heart ached once more, wishing Matt did not have to suffer a separation he never initiated.

As the young friends neared the door, they could hear Chrissy's parents arguing.

"*I don't want her hanging around with the son of a murderer!*" Chrissy's father yelled.

When Matt hung his head, Chrissy lifted it.

"I'm sorry he said that Matt. I don't care what he says. I know the real you."

The argument stopped when Chrissy entered the door.

"You think you're better than Matt's father, and you're not," Chrissy yelled at her father. "You're worse! A lot worse!"

Matt walked back to the car, buoyed by the words of Chrissy, knowing that despite the obstacles that lie ahead, he had someone who had not given up on him.

CHAPTER 51

Lance Dennison had kept himself in excellent shape. He did not smoke, rarely drank, and was addicted to exercise. DNA testing revealed that he used his superior conditioning to commit robberies and assaults against easy targets in and around Parables. His victims were now being notified that their perpetrator was found, and he would no longer be a threat.

The staff at Parables Hospital compiled the full history of Lance William Denison, including what he did to one of their own. It sparked controversy concerning a tradition that had always been held for organ donors: the staff honor guard.

In the end, it was decided the tradition would take place. The staff lined both sides of the hallway as the gurney holding Lance made its way to the surgical unit. Lance's mom walked behind the gurney, accompanied by the Director of the hospital. The sight of the staff honoring her wayward son touched her. When they neared the operating room, she broke down as she said her goodbye.

Lizzy stood between two nurses who held her arms. So many thoughts were running through her mind.

"*What happened?* Lizzy wondered. "*Why did this guy turn out the way he did?*"

There was a saying coined in Parables that seemed to speak to the occasion:

"Innocence is lost, one neglect at a time."

The staff continued to hold their position as Lance's mom trudged back down the hall with the Director. The honor guard was confirmation that she did the right thing.

Her only child had the good beaten out of him long ago. She had failed him, and the resulting damage eventually severed their relationship. It seemed that nothing good would ever come from him. The Director, the staff, the surgeons, the organ recipients, and Lance himself, were proving her wrong.

After Mrs. Dennison left the hospital, she went to a park about three miles away. It was in the older section of Parables, and it hadn't been updated yet. The wooden baby swings were still intact. She went to the one that was Lance's favorite. She closed her eyes and heard his laughter when she pushed him higher and higher. There were other rides, but Lance only wanted this swing. She wrapped her arms around the swing, hugging a moment in her mind, weeping until she was shaking. Then, letting go, she dropped to her knees, looked to the sky, and begged for forgiveness.

****

An ambulance was waiting for Lance's organs. A young father who was forty-four and had three children was going to receive his heart. His kidneys would allow two victims to be free from the need for dialysis. Parts of Lance would head in multiple directions, giving several people an opportunity for a better life.

Later that day, the mortuary manager broke protocol and allowed Lizzy and Ben to see Lance's body. She pulled out the slider from the refrigerated container, and gently lowered the blanket. The surgeons and morgue did a good job of making Lance look presentable, despite the surgical procedures.

"Evil on ice," Ben said.

It was a crude comment, but Ben was just expressing his feelings. Together they peered at the remains of a man who came close to ending their dreams but now provided the resources for other people to live out theirs. The mortuary worker gently covered the corpse back up and closed the compartment. Lizzy took Ben's hand as they walked to the cafeteria.

"So where is his mom going to spread the ashes?" Ben asked.

Lizzy looked up from her cup of coffee.

"In the Grand Canyon. Apparently, it was his favorite place to visit."

Ben shook his head. One of the most beautiful places in the world would soon be contaminated with the ashes of a derelict, a twisted hero, simply because he checked a box on the application for his driver's license.

Sometimes the world just did not make any sense.

****

Tony pushed the wheelchair holding Olivia and his son. Olivia's parents followed close behind. As they exited the hospital, Officer Riley was standing next to his police car. He motioned for Tony to come over. Olivia watched as Tony and Riley conversed. Their expressions were serious.

"Did the judge have a change of heart?" Olivia wondered. *"Would Tony be charged after all?"*

Eventually, Riley climbed into his car and drove away. Tony returned to Olivia and her parents.

"What's going on?" Olivia asked.

"The guy I got into the fight with, Rick, is dead," Tony said somberly.

Tony gave everyone the full story once they arrived home.

"Thank God!" Olivia said. "Now we can get on with our lives without worrying about him."

Tony gave her a halfhearted smile. The man who killed Tabby was gone. But he left behind a wife and a ten-year-old son. The whole mess left Tony with an empty feeling that he was indirectly responsible for Rick's death.

The feeling would stay with him; it would ensure he got the help he needed.

****

Officer Riley and Judge Logan dropped off their retirement papers together. The news spread rapidly throughout Parables and surrounding communities. The clerk who processed the forms was distraught. The two men in front of her were some of the last vestiges of better days.

"This town is going to miss you two." The clerk said sadly.

For their wives, the two-month notices were two months too long. As the final day arrived, there was a joint retirement party. A large number of people included faces from the past and present. Those who could not attend sent cards and gifts.

Discussions at the party included recent events with Lance Dennison. These discussions generated more questions than answers. In reality, for most people in Parables, the case of Lance Dennison had no answers.

As far as the town was concerned, it was a problem that took care of itself and left Parables a better place.

CHAPTER 52

Lizzy sat on the floor of her apartment, admiring her diploma. Ben was on his way over with Marge and Sam so they could all drive to dinner together. She closed her eyes, allowing herself to relax and revel in the moment.

She had almost fallen asleep when something gently pushed the diploma she was holding. As she slowly lowered it, there was Chance, looking at her. He seemed to be studying her eyes as if to ask, *"Can I trust you?"*

After a few seconds, Chance cautiously climbed into Lizzy's lap and laid down. Ben suddenly opened the door and entered the apartment, with Sam and Marge close behind him. Lizzy signaled for them to keep quiet, and pointed to Chance. She waved for Ben to come and sit next to her.

Chance turned and looked as Ben approached. Ben slowly sat down, as Chance continued to lie on Lizzy's lap.

"Well, it looks like pizza from Gargano's," Sam whispered.

Ben and Lizzy relayed their preferences. Marge left with Sam, gently closing the door behind them.

Lizzy slowly moved her hand toward Chance. Chance closed his eyes, a reflex from a loving cat who desperately wanted to feel affection again. As Lizzy gently petted him, he became more relaxed.

Ben moved closer to Lizzy, and also slowly moved his hand toward Chance. Chance watched him; then he moved his head into Ben's hand.

"See Ben, he knows you! He knows you helped to save him!"

Chance closed his eyes and moved his head between Ben and Lizzy so each could continue to pet him. And then, certain that he was truly loved, it happened:

Chance got his "purr" back.

EPILOGUE

.... 1 year later

Ruth studied herself in the mirror as she brushed her hair, feeling nervous and excited at the same time. The sitter was due to arrive in 45 minutes, and Mark shortly after that.

She met Mark at the dog park. He was with his eight-year-old daughter Claire. They did not have a dog. Mark was hoping the visit would be a distraction for both of them. It was seven months since Mark's wife died of a sudden brain aneurysm. Claire drifted into a silent shell, unable to deal with the loss of her mom.

Rascal noticed Claire first. He broke away from his pack of friends and sat down next to the little girl. She smiled when he nudged her with his nose, trying to get her to pick him up.

Ruth ran over to apologize when she noticed it; that look in Rascal's eyes. The look he had when he seemed to be searching for the little girl who had to leave him behind.

"I'm sorry he's bothering you," Ruth said, as she picked Rascal up. No sooner did she put him down, Rascal ran right back to Claire.

Claire smiled again at the inquisitive dog. Ruth extended her hand out to Mark.

217

"Hi, I'm Ruth." She said to Mark. "I think my dog is mistaking your daughter for someone he once knew."

After the brief introduction, Ruth told Mark and Claire about Rascal, and how his family had to leave him behind. The family had a little girl that looked a lot like Claire.

"Would you like to hold him?" Ruth asked Claire.

She nodded yes.

Rascal gave Claire a few kisses on her cheek, which made her giggle.

"What did you say his name was again?" Claire asked.

"Rascal," Ruth replied.

"Hi Rascal," Claire said.

Suddenly, Rascal started to squeal and whimper. His tail wagged furiously, as he smothered Claire with kisses. Claire broke out in laughter at the sudden rush of affection.

After that initial encounter, Mark and Ruth began to meet at the dog park almost every day, so that the friendship between Claire and Rascal would not be disrupted. While Claire sat and talked to Rascal about her mom, Mark and Ruth would chat about the turmoil and grief in their own lives.

One day Claire asked Ruth if she would like to go to a Mother's Day luncheon at her school. After clearing it with Mark, Ruth told Claire she would be honored to go.

They had a great time.

Mark was happy to see that Claire was engaging in life again. He loved watching Ruth and Claire talking with one another, and planning their next lunch or shopping day. Mark and Ruth also started to take turns inviting one another over for dinner. This development soon had Ruth's parents asking for regular "updates."

After their dinners, Claire and Rascal snuggled together and fell asleep. Mark and Ruth would then retire back to the kitchen, so they could talk. The conversations were easy but guarded.

It was on a beautiful fall day during one of their shopping trips, Claire slipped her hand into Ruth's hand as they walked among the shops in historical Stillwater. It happened naturally, a progression from a young girl's heart, who would never forget her mom, but still needed the affection that her mom had once provided.

A warm feeling went through Ruth as she held Claire's hand. But that night, she worried. She did not want the relationship to continue to grow if there was a possibility it might end and send Claire into a tailspin. The next day, she told Mark about the shopping trip, and that her relationship with Claire was now more than just a friendship.

Mark smiled.

"Next to Rascal, you're her favorite topic of conversation. She still talks about her mom. But she knows her mom cannot be here for her now. She believes that God sent you and Rascal to help look after her. So, your suspicions are right, you could say she's fallen hard for you."

Mark paused and took a deep breath. Ruth braced herself.

"And I have too," Mark said. "I know we agreed we need time to heal from our wounds before considering a serious relationship. And I know I'm still not completely through the grieving process. But I shudder to think where Claire and I would be right now if you and Rascal had not come into our lives. And the thought of not having you in our lives…"

Mark trailed off, unable to continue. Ruth wrapped her arms around him, relieved that her worries were unfounded.

So, tonight was an "experiment." She and Mark were going out on a date, alone, while Claire and Rascal would spend the night at Ruth's house. She placed the money out for the sitter and ordered a pizza delivery for later that evening.

The doorbell rang, and Ruth was slightly miffed that her preparation time was interrupted. She walked briskly to the door as she finished putting on her second earring.

She studied the face through the peephole and opened the door.

"Hello, Officer Riley," Ruth said, apprehensively.

"Citizen Riley," he said with a smile. I'm wondering if you have a few minutes. I was asked to give you some news."

Ruth invited him in, and as he sat down, Rascal ran up with a toy in his mouth. Riley threw the toy, and Rascal took off after it.

"I better put him in the kitchen, or he'll have you doing that all night," Ruth said. "It's time for his dinner anyway. I'll be right back."

Ruth tried to think of what possible news Riley would need to tell her. He did not seem upset, so it could not be too bad. She set Rascal's food bowl down and went back to the living room, where she sat across from Riley.

"It looks like you have plans, so I'll make this quick," Riley said. "Where to begin...well, back when Olivia was in the hospital, she struck up a friendship with a nurse who took care of her. You met her briefly."

Ruth nodded, wondering where this was going.

"Well, the nurse got married to this nice guy, and she recently found out she is pregnant. The nurse decided that both she and her husband needed some practice, so they began to babysit Tony and Olivia's son."

"Officer Riley, I mean .... why would I need to hear this news?" Ruth said. "Did you forget I agreed to leave them alone?"

Riley held his hand up.

"I'm getting to the point. Olivia was busy one day, and she asked Tony to pick up the baby. When he arrived, the baby was asleep. Sleeping next to him was a cat that belonged to the nurse. Tony picked up the baby and put him in his car seat. As he did this, he studied the cat. The nurse asked what was wrong. Tony said that the cat looked a lot like his mom's cat, whose name was Tabby."

Ruth sat forward in her chair.

"Well, as soon as Tony said the name Tabby, the cat woke up and rose to his feet. Tony said "Tabby" again, and the cat tilted his head and walked slowly toward him. He allowed Tony to pet him, but when he went to pick him up, the cat hobbled away into another room. Tony and the nurse got to talking, and put two and two together. The injury to the leg, the missing front claws, and files at the veterinarian's office confirmed what Tony was thinking."

"It's Tabby?" Ruth asked in astonishment.

Riley nodded.

"Anyway, that took longer than I planned. You're obviously in a hurry. I was asked to deliver this to you."

Ruth opened the bag Riley handed her. Inside was a picture of a cat being held by the nurse and her husband on their wedding day. Ruth smiled as a tear ran down her cheek. She could see it was Tabby.

"I better be going," Riley said.

Ruth walked him to the door, as Rascal barked in the background. She hugged Riley and thanked him for the picture. Riley smiled as he looked at Ruth.

"I have to admit, you look a hundred times better than when we first met at the side of the road! Did you ever get those batteries replaced?"

They both laughed when Ruth admitted she had not.

"You look great Ruth. I hope the guy you're getting ready for knows how lucky he is. Keep taking care of yourself."

Ruth waved as Riley drove away. Rascal was waiting impatiently for Ruth to release him from the kitchen. He ran into the living room carrying a toy, frantically looking for Riley.

Ruth placed the picture on her nightstand, and retrieved Tabby's collar from her purse. She draped the collar over the picture, a remnant of the dark past that was now replaced by a bright future.

She had to hurry now; the tears had smeared her make-up. She would wait until tomorrow to tell her parents the news. As she looked in the mirror, Ruth liked what she saw, and how she felt. There was a happiness building within her, that just moments before she might have blocked, or stifled, or deemed unmerited. That happiness was now given the freedom to expand…

The barriers had just been shattered.

ACKNOWLEDGEMENTS

This is the section of the book where the author expresses gratitude for those who were instrumental in the successful completion of his or her project. These individuals may not be familiar to you, which is too bad, since you would be blessed to have them in your life in any capacity. And if you are extremely lucky, you have them as friends and family.

There was **Michelle Rosas**, an extremely talented writer, author, and editor who selflessly share her time and knowledge throughout this process. Michelle was there in the beginning, reviewing the first draft and several afterward. If this novel was a sculpture, Michelle showed me where to take the chisel and correct the flaws I did not see, remove the redundancy (reduce 20 eyes to just 2), and refine the image so that the story was not sidetracked by unnecessary or irrelevant information (a kilt on the statue of David). She provided information on publishing, cover design, and other crucial steps in the completion of a novel. And all along the way, Michelle was a cheerleader, encouraging me to keep going when doubts were holding me back. In the end, I realize she was also my teacher, leaving me with skills that enhanced and improved my writing abilities. Like all good teachers, she gave me the confidence to go forward, to be brave, and as she said, "release it to the world." To say I am abundantly indebted to her is a gross understatement.

And there was **Charlene Lashier**, whose reviews included her impressions on the logic and flow of the story. She provided the feedback I needed from a skilled set of independent eyes. Her observations and questions led me to reorganize some chapters, make additional editorial changes, and improve character development. Most importantly, Charlene's feedback triggered changes and enhancements I realized were needed to improve the storyline. This would not have happened if Charlene did not take the time to do a comprehensive review and give critical feedback (both positive and negative) that every author desperately needs. But Charlene has always been about quality in everything she does. Like Michelle, I am most fortunate to have her as a close friend, willing to share her talents and join me on this journey.

The final member of my editorial team was **Gail Parry**. Gail was the "fine tooth comb" who I asked to do a final review of my completed manuscript. I worked with Gail for many years in the Regulatory Audit Division of U.S. Customs and Border Protection. Gail used her skills to review reports for professionals notoriously known for having horrendous writing abilities – Auditors. Her task was crucial since our reports were needed to support findings that involved substantial revenue recoveries and had the potential to go to court for resolution. Errors, omissions, or poorly written narratives made the difference between a highly polished report or one that jeopardized a potential settlement. Gail has not lost her touch. Her review uncovered several errors I overlooked. Her positive feedback on how the story impacted her also assured me that the manuscript was finally ready.

I want to thank my beta readers who read the early drafts and provided their feedback. My daughter **Sara Nicholson** was one of the first. Sara is a prolific reader who took time from her busy life as a nurse to read the crappy rough draft. Though numerous edits and changes were still to come, she was able to provide feedback on the plot. Her claim that it held her interest and attention was proven when she finished the draft in 2 days.

My wife **Susan** read several of the early drafts and provided notes with her thoughts and observations. She and my sister-in-law **Karla Hanley**, both retired nurses, pointed out some errors in the medical procedures I included in the story. They had a professional disagreement on what "blood type" I should use for the emergency surgery situation. When both dug in their heels and held their ground, I did what any good author does when his two experts have different opinions.

I flipped a coin.

My daughter **Chrissy Campbell Nicholson** was a final beta reader. More importantly, she provided professional assistance with the website development and marketing initiatives. With her skills in both disciplines, I had an expert to help me navigate the two toughest parts of a book project once it is completed. In exchange, I will routinely walk her dogs Maui and Bodhi, while she and her husband Tim tend to our grandson, Oliver.

Made in the USA
Monee, IL
20 May 2023

34144467R00135